EVEN MORE
NORTH DEVON
HISTORY

Peter Christie

EDWARD GASKELL *publishers*
DEVON

Edward Gaskell *publishers*
6 Grenville Street
Bideford
Devon
EX39 2EA

ISBN 1-898546-30-4

EVEN MORE
NORTH DEVON
HISTORY

Typset, printed and bound by
Lazarus Press
Unit 7 Caddsdown Business Park
Bideford
Devon
EX39 3DX

FOREWORD

Welcome to this, the third volume of my collected essays. The Foreword in Volume 1 explained how these articles came to be written for those who are interested. Most of the pieces in this volume appeared from 1988 to 1992 when publication halted and, as before, they cover a very wide range both in terms of subject and time periods. The last, long article is an edited version of the unpublished text of an essay I wrote in 1980 for the Bruce Oliver Essay Competition run by the North Devon Athenaeum.

As previously I have to thank the staffs of the North Devon Record Office and the North Devon Athenaeum especially Marjorie Snetzler for all her help with photocopying. Thanks are also due to Eddie Gaskell and his staff for all their assistance in actually seeing my typescript through to print.

I must also thank all those people who bought the first two books (and my others) and wrote to me (c/o the Publisher) commenting on the stories and often adding details I wasn't aware of before. I had expected this to be the last volume in this series even though there are still around 200 articles yet to be republished but in August of this year the editor of the Journal asked me to restart my series of contributions - so who knows - a fourth volume could eventually appear though I'm not sure what the title could be!

Peter Christie

Contents

Contents

Contents

List of illustrations

PEOPLE

1. FASCINATING RECORDS

Among the glories of British archives are the parish registers. Dating from a law passed in 1538, they list the baptisms, marriages and burials of most of our ancestors. A typical one comes from Parkham, near Bideford, and an examination of its first hundred years' worth of entries reveals some fascinating history.

The baptismal entries number about 1,200 over that period and list many names still found locally today, examples being Chope, Pickard and Galsworthy. Although the surnames are recognisable many of the Christian names are decidedly odd. What are we to make of Ebot Spyser and Emmot Shepheard, both christened in the early 1540s? Equally strange to modern ears are children called Arminall, Pressellay, Marfet, Harkiles, Onesimus and Redigon.

Certain names crop up more than once, suggesting local family linkages. One of these is Dorettia, a female name, while another is Pascho and its variants. This later occurs no less than 14 times over the hundred years and must have given rise to some confusion in such a small village.

Interestingly, the baptismal entries give only the father's name. Women appear only when the child is 'base born' or, as it is called in one entry, a 'basstert'. Some 15 illegitimate children's births are registered – a rate of just over one per cent. Compare this with our current figure of between 30 and 50 per cent.

In a few entries, additional information is given about the parents' occupation. Thus, the upper classes are indicated by the word 'gent' attached to their entry. John Horn is listed as 'the smith' in several entries while a Suzan, baptised in 1629, is noted as being the daughter of 'a pedler' and Jone, christened in 1630, as being the child of 'an Irish' (sic).

The marriage entries give minimal information, consisting as they do of just the bride and groom's names and the date of the wedding, although an occasional 'widow' is noted and sometimes the fact that a licence had been taken out for the marriage rather than having the banns called.

The years 1605 to 1628 are illegible owing (as we are told by a later rector) to 'the erosion of the surface of the parchment by rubbing with pumice stone to facilitate writing thereon' and the subsequent use of inferior quality ink.

Of the ones that are readable it is clear that certain months were most favoured. Of the 233 marriages, 40 took place in January, 34 in October and 33 in November – with none at all in March and minimal numbers in September and December. This odd distribution reflects three factors – the harvest timetable, the church year and local folk beliefs. Thus Easter and Christmas were times to avoid while in September everyone was too busy harvesting the crops.

The burial entries are similar in that very little detail is given about those buried other than names and date. Occasionally there is an addition as in 1540 when 'an Irish woman' known simply as Katherine is buried.

The average annual number of interments over these 100 years is about seven, though in 1564 there were 23 – 14 in September and October, which suggests an outbreak of some fatal disease. This explanation might also apply to 1546 when there were nine burials, of which seven were in July. These exceptional years should be compared with at least five other years when only one burial took place.

These illustrations of what can be gained from a study of our parish register can be found from all such records. Every parish has them and they help illuminate the 'simple annals' of our forefathers' lives – and, of course, they are still of use today though the local registry office has lessened their importance greatly.

North Devon Journal 6.8.1992

2. NORTH DEVONIANS WHO WILLED IT AWAY IN YEARS LONG PAST

All wills have to be 'proved' before legacies can be paid and heirs inherit. In the past before this occurred an inventory or list of the deceased person's goods had to be produced. Most date from the seventeenth century but in Devon's case very few survived the 1942 bombing of Exeter. Of the 500 or so that did about a quarter refer to North Devonians and fascinating they are.

All classes are represented – from Grace Beaple of Barnstaple who left property worth some £385 to poor John Whytfyld of Landkey whose worldly goods totalled just £4.55. Many differing occupations are also found – weaver, husbandman, shoemaker and butcher to name but four.

The true interest of such inventories, however, lies in the goods listed, often room by room, that our ancestors owned. Mistress Beaple mentioned above, who died in 1650, left 'Jewels and Rings', coral and pearl bracelets, gold chains and a 'piece of Barbery gold' worth some £65 along with £80 worth of 'wearinge apparrell' – a very expensively dressed lady.

John Quirke of Braunton died around the same time and although it is not stated was evidently a farmer. He had, for example, £3 worth of 'Corne in the barne' as well as 'Corne in the ground' worth a further pound. His clothing was only costed at £2.66, rather different to Grace Beaple.

A farmer on a larger scale was John Cawker of Holsworthy. His inventory dated 1666 details 8 oxen, 10 'kine', 42 steers and heifers, 7 'Labour Horses' and 7 colts, 112 sheep and 6 pigs as well as geese and ducks. He also owned 5 ploughs and 2 harrows. In his house were pewter dishes and brass implements all of which added up to nearly £800.

One of the most interesting lists is that for Nicholas Cooke of Barnstaple, an apothecary or chemist which is dated 1695. Amongst his furniture were 22 'Rushian Leather Chairs' and 8 'playne Leather Chaires' – from his waiting room perhaps? As befitting a man of learning he also owned 'One old large Mapp of the world' valued at five shillings (25p).

Cooke's total belongings were valued at £81.12 – very different from poor (but grandly named) Bartholomew Bugsleigh of Arlington who died in 1646. His total estate was judged to be worth just £7.67 of which £6 was 'Money owinge him'. One hopes his heirs got their money!

An especially sad inventory is that of the oddly named Scipio Haywood of Winkleigh who committed suicide around 1677. He was relatively rich what with his cider press, silver cutlery and 'Fower Chamber pottes of tyn'. Even the rich, however, became unhappy enough to take their own life. In this case his goods passed by custom to the 'King's Great Almoner' then the Bishop of Winchester.

If you are interested in reading more about these inventories the full text of some 266 Devon ones is given in Volume II of the Devon & Cornwall Record Society published in 1966 and available in local libraries.

North Devon Journal 15.9.1988

3. VILLAGERS WHO LOOKED AFTER THEIR OWN

Most of my stories concern unusual events – events that made news in the past make good reading today. Occasionally, however, one comes across true human interest stories that weren't newsworthy in their day but are fascinating today.

Around 1754 one Benjamin Bowden, a 27 year old labourer from Bishops Nympton took the 'king's shilling' and joined the 37th Regiment of Foot. He served for two years in Captain Bowchier's company 'faithfully and honestly' until 'by loosing of his sight by lightning when on duty' he was discharged as unfit. This occurred at Chatham and as well as getting a Chelsea Hospital pension his Captain gave him a good reference to help him on his way home.

In April 1757, however, he was arrested in Somerset as 'a rogue and a vagabond.' Questioned by magistrates he gave his birth place as Bishops Nympton. Hearing this the court sent him back there as was the practice in those days – if a person became ill or couldn't work, their home parish gave 'relief' to them – provided they lived in that parish. Benjamin soon arrived home and apparently married.

Unfortunately the young invalid didn't settle down, if we are to judge from a letter sent to the War Office by the parish of Bishops Nympton. They pointed out that the ratepayers in the village had to support Benjamin as he couldn't work and asked if his pension could be sent direct to them 'for if paid to the said pensioner it will all be spent in debauchery and drunkeness within a few days it is received.'

This the War Office agreed to do which was just as well, for Benjamin lived to be 63 and with his wife had at least three children, all 'chargable' to the parish.

If one looks at the parish Overseer of the Poor accounts, one finds constant payments to Benjamin and his family. Thus in his first year home Benjamin received £1 'in Necessity.' In 1761 2s went to him 'in sickness' and in the same year a Temperance Cole was paid 1s 'for yielding up her house to Bowden' whilst a local carpenter got 11s to provide a bed for the blind ex-soldier. These payments continued until 1790 when we read 'for Benjamin Bowden's shroud 2s 8d for laying forth 1s 6d, for coffin 6s, bell and grave 2s, affadavit 6d' – this last being a sworn statement that Benjamin had been buried in a woollen shroud as was then the law.

One wonders what poor Benjamin did to pass his 33 years of blind life in this small Devon parish? Presumably once his pension was taken away his 'debauchery' stopped and he found something constructive to do – further research would probably reveal more about him and his family – and it would appear that he has left descendants in the area today.

A small unimportant human story perhaps but one of some interest to us today.

North Devon Journal 16.6.1988

4. REJECTED SUITOR TURNS TO SUICIDE

Human tragedies make sad reading – whenever they happened. In 1832 readers of the *Journal* would have come across a short paragraph concerning one Richard Tucker of Marwood.

Richard was a cabinet maker aged 24 who, as young men will, had fallen in love with a young woman in Marwood. As the report put it 'He had paid attention to a young woman of the village for a considerable time.' She had returned his affection at first but 'lately he had had reasons to believe that she favoured the addresses of another suitor.'

Poor Richard was provided with proof of this in a particularly public way. In March 1832, 'according to the annual custom on Lady Day' the young people of the village got together and held a dance 'in the club room of the public house.' Richard turned up but on arriving 'found his faithless nymph dancing with his rival.' Incensed he demanded to know what was going on but she 'treated him with scorn' – in front of all his fellow villagers. Richard was shattered and slunk out of the dance.

This might just have blown over and never have entered history's record but Richard went off and, as the contemporary reporter rather brutally put it, 'put an end to his existence by hanging himself.' Not only did he go off and commit suicide but he chose to hang himself from a beam in a stable which was actually underneath the club room where he had been publicly humiliated. This was a ghoulish touch as whilst he was dying his cruel sweetheart was dancing overhead in the arms of another.

In such a case as this obviously there had to be an inquest and a coroner's jury was duly summoned. Not surprisingly they returned a verdict of suicide during 'temporary insanity.' A sad note in the *Journal* adds that Richard's mother 'died in similar manner about three years ago.'

Just to satisfy my own curiosity I checked the burials recorded in the Marwood parish register for 1832 and found Richard's burial. His mother Mary has also been buried there in February 1829, aged 65. I was heartened to see this as, even as late as the nineteenth century, suicides were still being buried in unconsecrated ground away from the churchyard – often at crossroads with a wooden stake through their heart! Clearly the inhabitants of Marwood weren't so heartless as others.

North Devon Journal 18.1.1990

5. MAN DIES AFTER OPERATION

In August 1841 Robert Page, 28 year old master of the Barnstaple National School died. Nothing remarkable in that perhaps except that at a coroner's inquest allegations were made that he died as a result of the actions of an itinerant doctor then in the town to treat deafness.

At the inquest Page's widow 'who was overcome with grief' recounted how her husband had told her he was going to see Dr Cronin who was advertising that he could cure the deaf. She advised him to wait and see if he was any good but he ignored her and went off for a consultation.

On his return he looked very ill and announced that he had undergone 'the operation.' The next day he continued to feel ill but returned to Cronin for a second treatment. This time his wife accompanied him and watched while the doctor put 'an instrument up his nostrils' and pumped air into his head.

Page went home very faint but returned for a third bout of treatment the next day. On all three visits he was given some ear drops as well. That evening he became very sick and suffered a violent nose-bleed and at his wife's insistence took some medicine prepared by another local doctor. Dr Cronin also came to see him and blamed his illness on the medicine and not his operations.

Page then became delirious constantly calling 'Pump the gas out of my head which you have pumped into it.' Within a day he was dead.

A Doctor Budd who gave evidence at the inquest thought the operation 'highly dangerous' and likened it to 'firing an air gun into the ear.' After this statement the jurors voted whether to order Cronin to give evidence or not but by 7 to 6 decided not to, and returned a verdict of 'Death from inflammation of the brain' but forbore to specify the cause.

Dr Cronin did in fact defend himself in a letter to the *Journal* the following week. He claimed his treatment of Page for deafness had been successful and suggested that his patient had died of jaundice with complications. He also attacked Dr Budd as he was 'surprised that any one who knows anatomy should deem it a dangerous operation.'

He was supported by another letter the next week from a North Molton surgeon Dr Ley who reckoned the operation 'to be simple and effectual.' Ley, who stated that he had never met Cronin, felt constrained to defend him against unjust attacks and 'to wipe away the odium and mystification which has poured in upon an unoffending individual and a mostly valuable operation.' He further thought it unfair that Cronin hadn't been summoned to give his version of events to the inquest jury.

On this note the story ended. Poor Mrs Page was left a young widow with several young children while the public were left in a state of ignorance as to whether deafness could be cured by this method or not. Thank goodness for the NHS I say.

North Devon Journal 2.4.1992

6. BARNSTAPLE LADS TOOK ONE-LEGGED FIGURE OUT ON 'BIT OF A SPREE'

I have written before about how our ancestors reacted to misdemeanours by individuals in their midst – from the Buckland Brewer 'Mayor' (wife beating) to the 'Stag Hunts' (adultery) and from the Consistory Court (sexual impropriety) to the stocks (general misbehaviour). A new one to me, however, occurs in a Barnstaple Petty Sessions Court report from June 1849.

In that month two boys Daniel Nogle and William Cockram were arrested in the streets of Derby, Barnstaple by P.C. Snell. A third boy called James Buckingham was also arrested but he later made off. P.C. Snell had been called in by a Mrs Williams after a disgraceful spectacle took place and upset her.

Apparently there had been 'an occasion of public scandal, in the nature of Crim. con.' in the area a few days before. 'Crim con' is an abbreviation for criminal conversation and is a very old legal term for adultery – suggesting that one had held a conversation with a married man or woman of a 'criminal' nature i.e. against the laws of marriage.

Some of 'the juveniles of that vicinity commemorated this by a grotesque exhibition which they carried about the streets.' This took the form of a mannequin 'intended, it was said, to represent one of the parties compromised by the affair.'

The figure was 'attired in a marine dress, and boasted a wooden leg' – so it must have been fairly obvious to all the locals just who was being represented – one legged sailors weren't that common even then! Most of the inhabitants of Derby were amused but the proceedings got out of hand.

Nogle and Cockram were brought into court along with their model and all three were put in the 'prisoner's box' in the courtroom. Here the facts of the case were gone through and the boys asked to explain themselves. They replied that 'they were merely having a bit of a spree'. The magistrates answered this with the ruling 'that such fun could not be tolerated.'

This sounded harsh but the boys were only fined 1/- (5p) each plus costs and then dismissed so it is plain to see just where the bench's sympathies lay.

North Devon Journal 22.9.1988

7. TEACHER TRIES LANDLORD

Ever since the eighteenth century Newport has been the genteel end of Barnstaple, In 1850, however, a less than genteel event occurred there featuring William Cann, master of the local National or State School. In February of that year he took one William Baker, landlord of the Rose and Crown to court for 'using abusive and violent language to him.'

Cann alleged that Baker had not only abused him but also made 'imputations' over the school-master's relationship with a local married woman. The abuse had taken the form of Baker calling him 'a damned dirty snob' and 'a damned blackguard' but the only witness the school-master could produce was his own wife – and even she admitted that she had only heard part of Baker's conversation.

Cann added that someone had even paid the Town Crier to announce his alleged adultery around the town. The Crier, not unnaturally, had refused on the grounds of decency and Baker swore in court that he knew nothing about it. The magistrates decided to reserve their decision on these charges until the next case had been dealt with.

This case concerned three young men, John Brayley, Richard Chammings and John Buzzacott – summoned for parading effigies of him through Newport – an old custom designed to publicly humiliate a suspected adulterer. Cann knew that the crude models were meant to represent him as one had a stump for an arm and he, in fact, only had one hand.

Accompanied by a mob of youths beating tin kettles and shouting, the effigies were carried to a bonfire and there burnt to great cheering. The local policeman. P.C. Snell, supported Cann's evidence adding that this custom was known as Skibbeton Ridings, for some obscure reason.

The Mayor and his fellow magistrates then commented on the case – somewhat oddly highlighting the danger of carrying lighted objects through the streets next to thatched buildings! They added that they were determined to stamp out such behaviour and then only fined the three youths one shilling (5p) each, hardly a crushing fine.

In the same issue of the *Journal* that carried this report, there was an advertisement placed by the vicar of Newport and a group of local gentlemen publicly affirming their faith in Mr Cann's morality, though by then the damage had been done. Folk justice, like life, was rough in those days!

North Devon Journal 24.11.1988

8. SOCIETIES FOR TEETOTALLERS

Many Victorians liked a drink but many others joined teetotallers' societies to fight the 'demon alcohol.' One such was the South Molton Royal Albert Temperance Association which was rather unusual in that it had its own meeting hall given by a Mr.J.G.Pearse. In this the members held their AGMs and one was held in September 1863.

The meeting began with a 'social tea' and was followed by the business meeting. The annual report was first read by the secretary who reckoned that the year had been a great success. Twelve months previously they had been 'virtually defunct' and 'powerless to extend a helping hand to assist any inebriate out of the vile kennel into which so many of our fellow men had fallen.'

During the year, however, they had taken possession of their new hall and attracted some ninety people a week to attend. He guessed at the number of members but he thought that there were 450 'individuals who still refuse to touch, taste or handle the accursed thing.'

A Band of Hope (or youth section) was being formed and at least twenty members had enrolled themselves in the local Freehold Land Society. This latter connection is interesting as the Land Society provided allotments to those who 'signed the pledge' - a boon removed from two people who had 'broken the pledge and have been ejected.' The vacancies were filled by two others 'whose principles we trust, are more firmly fixed' as the secretary put it. At a time when incomes were low, such an incentive was of great value. The report was ended with a ringing call for members to do more 'to grapple with the most gigantic curse that ever befell a nation.'

He was followed by the Rev.Harding who said it was a shame that among a body of teetotallers numbering 450, the total income for the year was lower than expected.

The last speech came from John Lethaby, a sweep and reformed drunkard. He claimed that for more than two years 'he was without a coat or waistcoat, and often in the pursuit of his vocation had to travel in this semi-nude state in the winter season over the forest of Exmoor.' Since joining the association though he had been 'getting on pretty well' and 'wished his old companions would join him.'

One wonders if there is a need for such groups today or have we, as a nation and as individuals, conquered the 'gigantic curse' of drunkeness?

North Devon Journal 1.11.1990

9. A VILLAGE INSIGHT THROUGH THE CENSUS

Every ten years we, as a nation, fill in our census forms and after a century these censuses are made public. I have written before about the 1851 census for one North Devon town – but what of the villages?

Just over 140 years ago the inhabitants of Westleigh near Bideford sat down to fill in their official forms little realising that they were committing to paper a complete survey of their village for future historians to mull over. At that date there were 508 people living in the parish ranging in age from the 89 year old widow Sarah Holland to a child just two days old and yet to be named.

The population today hovers around 330. Such a drop is general for most North Devon villages with the disappearance of agricultural employment and large rural families.

Two households had nine family members but three were even

larger. At both Tapeley House and the vicarage there were 11 people under one roof though this included 12 servants between the two establishments. The largest grouping, however, was at the hamlet of Eastleigh where there were 12 people in the farmhouse of Robert Puddicombe.

Alongside these extended 'families' were the single person households. Mainly widows they included 72 year old Elizabeth Short and 77 year old Elizabeth Langdon, both noted as being 'paupers.'

If we look at the occupatiions listed we find the single largest group to be the ubiquitous 'agricultuaral labourer/farm servant.' The other groupings range from 'farmer' to 'Landed Proprietor' and include the whole range of old village craftsmen such as blacksmiths, carpenters, millers, masons, shoemakers and thatchers.

All of these, of course, were, male occupations. Women do, however, form one skilled group. Some 10 female 'glovers' are listed almost certainly being outworkers from the factories in Torrington and Bideford. Other female jobs include some dressmakers and nurses along with a couple of married school teachers.

One other group must be mentioned – the servants. Out of the total population of 508 some 72 people might be classed as servants – nearly 1 in 7 of the parish's inhabitants and a clear illustration of the prevalence of this job throughout Victorian Britain. In those days before labour saving devices had been introduced servants were very necessary to keep large households going – if you could afford them (though wages were laughably tiny). The oddest occupation listed was that for William Wood of Southcott Cottage who merely described himself as 'Citizen of the USA.'

The last piece of information the Westleigh Victorians noted was their birthplace. Many people today have a vague idea that our ancestors were born, married and died in just one village, but of the 508 inhabitants of Westleigh just 263 were born in the village – much higher than today but clearly showing that Victorian country dwellers were fairly mobile. Most of the 'incomers' came from the rest of North Devon but a few were from places further afield including Surrey, Yorkshire, Kent, Westmoreland, Jersey and Ireland.

Thus we have a picture of mid-nineteenth century Westleigh – a self-contained settlement of large families mostly working on the land with a sprinkling of more cosmopolitan people bringing new blood and ideas into the village.

North Devon Journal 10.9.1992

10. AMERICAN EXPLORES ON FOOT

It is always intriguing to discover what others make of us and our area. North Devon, because it was rather isolated, attracted few visitors in the past. One who did come, in 1864, was an American Elihu Burritt and he published his reactions in a rare book entitled *A Walk from London to Land's End and Back.*

He entered North Devon from Cornwall first encountering Hartland – a place name also found in his home state of Connecticut. Walking through the 'crooked and narrow streets' of the town, he describes the 'queer, yellow-faced, thatched cottages.' Stopping only for dinner he continued the 15 miles to Bideford and on his way fell in with Edward Capern.

Capern is better known as the 'Postman Poet' as he made up his poetry as he delivered letters in the Buckland Brewer area. He made a tremendous impression on Burritt as he was an ordinary working man made good, a character out of American mythology. Indeed, Burritt spent some days with him travelling in the ponycart.

On one day he and the poet were near Buckland Brewer when a voice yelled out 'Oi zay! baint yur gwoin ter stop an tak a drop?' Needless to say they did, joining a local farmer and his workgang drinking 'homebrew' from a 'wood-bottomed cow's horn' and singing some of Capern's songs.

It was on this journey that they met 'Old Blind Tom' near Littleham. Everyday this old man carried a half-hundred-weight sack of coal on his back from Bideford some three miles for just one penny. Poor Tom, who was about 65, was deaf as well as blind but he still kept himself on his rather thankless labour, refusing to ever enter the workhouse.

Burritt visited the Westward Ho! pebble ridge, terming it a 'necklace of blue, white veined cornelians, two miles in length, 50 feet wide and 20 feet deep.'

He also attended two religious services on the Sunday with a visit to Old Town Cemetery in Bideford to see the grave of Capern's only daughter (now shamefully neglected and vandalised).

The American traversed a long path with 'cold rocky' Exmoor to the north and farmland to the south on his way to Somerset. A fleeting visit to North Devon perhaps but one that gives us entertaining glimpses of some old Devonian characters and scenes.

North Devon Journal 20.6.1991

11. WHEN SNOW BROUGHT A DEATH IN THE LANES

Snow always seems to catch the British unawares. In North Devon roads are closed, businesses halt and whole communities are cut off regularly by snow storms. Luckily, however, few lives are lost owing to the courage of our rescue services. But this was not the case in earlier centuries...as a sad case in 1873 shows.

One morning at the beginning of February, Parracombe schoolmaster, John Lock, the district registrar of births, marriages and deaths, set off for Barnstaple. His intention was to deliver copies of the various registers he kept to the local superintendent registrar. Unforseen business kept him longer than he anticipated and by the time he left in the late afternoon snow was already falling.

He had twelve miles to walk and, armed with a stout stick, seemed to make good time. Early in the evening he called at the Foxhunter's Inn, Loxhore, where he chatted with his friend William Delve the local blacksmith.

He mislaid his stick and a man called Pugsley went outside and found it for him. By this time snow was falling heavily but the school-master told his friends not to worry as 'he should soon get home.' He set off but never arrived.

Next morning Arthur Smyth, a crippled youth of Parracombe, was out walking in the sparkling white landscape when he came upon a snow-covered mound in the middle of Minnemoor Lane. Thinking this odd he prodded it with his crutch and 'laid bare a man's hand.' Overcoming his shock he hobbled for help and William Bourn, the local policeman came, identified the body and removed it to Lock's house.

Poor Lock was dead and stiff – through both the cold and rigor mortis. In his hands were clenched fistfuls of snow as though he had made last desperate efforts to force his way through the deep drifting snow. A Dr. Fairbank of Lynton was called in to certify death.

At the inquest he reckoned that Lock, who was 49, had been overcome with fatigue, collapsed and frozen to death. As his registrar's job 'sometimes required him to walk as much as 25 miles after his school hours' such a theory obviously had some truth in it. The inquest jury found the cause of death to be 'accidental.'

The following week a letter was published in all the North Devon newspapers from the Rev. P. N. Leakey, rector of Parracombe. This was an appeal for funds to help support Lock's widow as 'she is left totally unprovided for and is too delicate to earn her own livelihood.' This appeal raised a small sum which probably helped but couldn't take the place of her poor husband.

Such was life and death in North Devon a hundred years ago.
North Devon Journal-Herald 18.4.1985

12. DRINK AND DRUGS IN VICTORIAN BARNSTAPLE

Readers of the *Journal* in May 1873 must have been shocked when they read the story accompanying the headline 'Melancholy end of a young lady of Barnstaple.' The story concerned a local schoolmistress who died of opium eating and alcoholism – not the usual end for Victorian teachers!

At the end of April 1873 Robert Bailey, a shipwright of Appledore, had sailed to Heanton Punchardon to collect a cargo of timber. Whilst there he noticed a body washed up on the beach and recovered it with the aid of a boathook. It was taken to Braunton mortuary where it was identified as that of Miss Elizabeth Hutchings, 'a young woman of highly respectable parentage,' from Barnstaple.

At the inquest the coroner's jury heard a bizarre story which didn't quite fit the girl's respectable background. The first witness was her landlady, Mary Ireland of Raleigh, with whom Elizabeth had lived for three years. She told the court how her lodger had run a small boarding school in partnership with her aunt, Mrs Maxwell, in Barnstaple High Street. The aunt had remarried and given up her share in the school to her niece.

Mrs Ireland ended by stating that Elizabeth had 'been in the habit for years of taking opium' but nevertheless she 'was a very clever woman and occupied her time with crochet work and reading.'

Mr. R. P. Morrison, a local surgeon-dentist who had known Elizabeth for a long time, painted a sad picture of her. After her aunt's marriage Elizabeth became 'greatly given to drink and opium eating, and gradually disposed of all her furniture and effects.' On one occasion she wandered off and was found under a hedge at Combe Martin, being bought back in a cart by the police. At this period she 'would drink anything she could get' including, apparently, surgical spirits.

Clearly incapable of looking after herself she was placed in the North Devon Infimary by her friends. Here she stayed 18 months but the committee 'thinking it was not a fit case for the charity, she was compelled to leave.' It was at this point that Mrs Ireland took her under her wing.

John Hames of Barnstaple, a chemist, next appeared and recounted how Elizabeth had come to his shop at least twice a week to buy opium. The drug 'was her life' he said, adding, 'I have sold as much as a quarter of an ounce daily for her.' She also apparently visited other chemists for extra supplies.

The jury returned a verdict of 'Found drowned' which, at least, did not add the stain of suicide to poor Elizabeth's already besmirched character.

North Devon Journal 11.4.1985

13. SAD TALE OF A RUNAWAY

One night in mid-September 1873 the streets of the Derby area of Barnstaple were thronged with hundreds of angry people 'exhibiting the most awful violence in their language and threats to Mr Brown and his family which they followed up by breaking almost all the glass in the windows of his house.'

Who was the unfortunate Mr Brown? The story begins at the start of September that year when Thomas Brown, a Barnstaple mason, went to the police station to report that his 18 year old apprentice William Burgess had run away, breaking his indenture agreement. Mr Brown thought he had gone to Liverpool to emigrate to the USA as thousands of Britons were then doing.

A warrant was issued and the unlucky William was arrested in Liverpool and brought back to appear before magistrates. This was unfortunate as his mother and the rest of his family were embarked and ready to sail to join his father in the USA. The father had gone over several years earlier looking for work and had at last raised the fare for his family.

When the money came William was in the third year of his apprenticeship and earning 7s 6d (37½p) a week. His mother had pleaded with Mr Brown to let her son go but he refused – as he was legally entitled to do so. It may have been legal but the family's friends didn't think much of the finer points of the law which is why they attacked poor Brown's house.

The police managed to disperse the mob 'but did not succeed in detecting any of those who threw stones' – an unlikely failure. One can only guess that their sympathies lay with the crowd. The report of the disturbance noted that the 'conduct of many women in the riotous assembly was most outrageous.'

When the apprentice appeared in court soon afterwards the room was packed with his supporters but the magistrates were not to be intimidated by numbers. They said that normally they would not tolerate the breaking of apprenticeship indentures but that this was an exceptional case. They therefore fined William £5 with 14 days to pay or three months in gaol (and this was lenient!).

Poor William could not pay of course but a benefactor, J. P. S. Marshall of the 'Old Bank' paid the fine. The newspaper editor added 'We hear the boy has since obtained another situation in the town and will remain there till a further communication is received from his father.'

In fact he very quickly returned to Liverpool and joined an emigrant ship and so went to establish another North Devon link with the New World – and he certainly went with a bang!
North Devon Journal-Herald 16.5.1985

14. COMMITMENTS OF FATHERHOOD ARE FOREVER

The recent call by the Government to make the fathers of illegitimate children more financially responsible for their offspring is nothing new. In the last century, courts had the power to make affiliation orders on recalcitrant fathers, whereby they were ordered to pay so much per week towards the upkeep of their children. The workings of this scheme meant that fathers were often dragged to court and the whole, often sorry, story brought into the glare of publicity.

One such court case occurred in Barnstaple in May 1880 when Thomas Mortimer, an engine driver was charged by Henrietta Bailey as being the father of her child. The child had actually been born in January 1879 but soon after its birth Thomas had left Barnstaple and had only just returned.

Henrietta, it was said, was a servant girl who 'had lived from time to time in respectable service.' Whilst working at the Clarence Hotel in Ilfracombe she had met Thomas and struck up an 'improper intimacy.' Thomas promised her marriage but then disappeared. Henrietta presented her evidence to the court and her mother also appeared to swear that Thomas had indeed promised marriage.

Thomas hired a lawyer to represent him and this gentleman carried out a searching cross-examination of Henrietta designed to show her in the worst light possible. Was it not true that she had two other illegitimate children and not by Thomas? Yes it was true. Was it also true that she was in fact a prostitute and that it was therefore impossible to establish the paternity to Thomas?

Naturally Henrietta strongly denied this, but John Darch was called as a witness and he swore 'from his own knowledge' that Henrietta was a prostitute.

In this case, Henrietta's character was besmirched, her mother was presumably revealed as a perjuror and both Thomas and Darch were identified as men who apparently frequented prostitutes.

Her lawyer pointed out that Darch's evidence only applied to his client some 12 months previous to the birth of the child and that she had presumably stopped following her 'trade' when she met Thomas.

The court eventually reached their decision and Thomas was ordered to pay 1/6 a week 'until the child should have attained the age of 13' plus court costs.

Do we wish to return to this public laundering of personal dirty washing? It is hard to see how we can avoid it if we do embrace this particular Victorian value.

North Devon Journal 29.3.1990

15. DEVONIAN BELIEF IN THE POWERS OF WITCHCRAFT

December 1885 saw the death of Thomas Western of Prixford Barton aged 82. The old gentleman had left a will disposing of some £4000 of property (then a large sum) to his second wife Mary. Nothing unusual in all this of course and perhaps nothing too unusual in the fact that the will was disputed by the 8 children of his first marriage who were left nothing.

The case went to the High Court where its hearing revealed some bizarre beliefs. It came out that up until a few years before his death Thomas had been on excellent terms with all his children and had promised them all a legacy. In 1880 his first wife died and he remarried. As so often happens, the children fell out with their stepmother.

In March 1883 Thomas developed a severe case of eczema on his hands – an illness which he blamed on 'the power of witchcraft.' Thomas reckoned it was his children who were bewitching him and wrote to Exeter to consult the 'white witch' there who was reckoned to be the high priest of good magic in Devon. This 'mystic authority' agreed that witchcraft was to blame for the eczema and that it was caused by two people; one, a woman who lived nearby and two, a member of his own family. They could be recognised because one was a 'crab' and the other would 'come three times running to Mr Western's house.'

Thomas concluded that his daughter Ellen was the 'crab' as she was deformed and that another of his daughters Maria must be the other woman as she visited his house three times. He told his doctor of his suspicions but his doctor merely scoffed at him. Thomas, however, stuck to his belief and disinherited all his children.

At the court hearing, various witnesses were called, including his doctor, a local bank manager and a local solicitor, all of whom testified to their client's sound mental condition. They all agreed, however, that Thomas 'unquestionably' believed in witchcraft.

The lawyers in the case got together at the direction of the judge and came to a compromise solution. The property was to go to the stepmother for the rest of her life, but was to revert to the children after her death.

People alive today might well remember Western's children whom he accused of witchcraft. His beliefs are almost certainly still shared by some Devonians today.

North Devon Journal 14.6.1990

16. ONE DOSE TOO MANY FOR DOCTOR

Doctors are generally regarded as pillars of society – examples to the rest of us perhaps – whose lives should be beyond reproach. In May 1891, however, Dr. John Day of Torrington appeared before the magistrates of the Bideford Borough Police Court on three charges – assault, threatening behaviour and drunkeness.

The charges were brought by his wife who was legally separated from him and living in lodgings in Elm Grove, Bideford.

On the evening of May 4 Dr Jones came to her lodgings and barged his way in. He grabbed her claiming that 'he had a policeman at the end of the road and was going to put her into the workhouse.' The landlady then appeared and distracted his attention long enough for Mrs Jones to escape into the sitting room. Her husband followed her, however, threatening to cut her throat.

At this point in the evidence the judge asked how long they had been separated. She answered seven years 'during which time she had lived at Torrington, London and Bideford.' Dr Jones had agreed to pay her 35p a week maintenance money but he often didn't pay.

Dr Jones' lawyer then asked a few questions. Wasn't it true that if her money didn't arrive she went to Torrington and walked up and down outside her husband's surgery sending him 'irritating messages?' A letter she had written threatening him with prison unless he paid up was also read out.

Other witnesses then appeared including the landlady Sarah Barry who claimed that the doctor was drunk when he came to her house. Her next door neighbour, one J. Spencer alleged that he saw Dr Jones fall over in the garden and not get up until helped by a policeman – as he was 'so drunk.'

The defence lawyer rather feebly said that 'his client was a man given to eccentricities of conduct.' He had only come to Bideford to see a patient and had gone on to see his wife over a letter she had written which he found offensive. He wasn't drunk when he saw his wife and he only fell down in the garden as he 'suffered from heart disease.'

This rigmarole didn't impress the bench very much and they summarily fined the good doctor £1 for the assault and bound him over to keep the peace in the sum of £25. On the charge of drunkeness the magistrates listened to evidence from three local policemen and rapidly added an extra 50p fine to the one already given.

Dr. Jones paid and departed leaving us with the thought that perhaps the far more flexible divorce laws we have today aren't such a bad thing after all.

North Devon Journal 6.6.1991

17. MAGICAL WAY OF CURING

One topic I return to now and again seems to be of perennial interest – magic. On several occasions I have written about the white (and black) witches and wizards of North Devon who, though often calling themselves cattle doctors, nevertheless were best known as human magicians.

Some of the most famous Devonian practitioners came from South Devon but often travelled to the north for business. One of the last of these was also one of the most famous. This was a Mr Tuckett of Exeter who in the last decades of the last century regularly came to the Bell Inn at Parkham to carry on his trade.

One story concerns a Mr Bale of Littleham, a farmer, who asked Tuckett to help his ewes which were miscarrying. Tuckett reckoned the farmer had been 'overlooked' (bewitched), so he gave him a bag containing a piece of paper to wear around his neck at night. Such pieces of paper usually had a suitable verse or two from the Bible written on them. He also recommended that he got a new ram.

In other cases where farmers considereed themselves to be bewitched the wizard would give them a bag of stones and tell them to throw some water in the direction of the supposed witch saying 'I do it in the name of Tuckett.'

One of the main cures Tuckett carried out was to remove warts by counting the number to be removed and writing the total in dust on the ground. This is an example of a very ancient art known as 'sympathetic magic.' As the dust blew away and disappeared so the warts would also go. Many still do this today using a piece of bacon fat or banana.

A white witch, Mrs Dovell of Countisbury was famed for curing illness and stopping bleeding. She removed warts by touching them with her wedding ring and saying a few words. Such magic could, however, be countered and the landlord of the Blue Ball, one Jim Smith, once turned the tables on Mrs Dovell.

One Sunday when the old lady was praying in church he banged an iron nail into one of her footprints in the churchyard clay. This was an old trick, which, allegedly, made it impossible for Mrs Dovell to get up off her knees until the nail was removed.

Do we believe such things today? Well, wart charmers are still in great demand – and they work – so who are we to scorn such old practices? White witches and wizards still exist in North Devon though perhaps they don't have such formidable 'public' reputations as they once did.

North Devon Journal 8.4.1991

18. CHILDREN WHO WERE LEFT TO A BABY FARMER

Today the death of a child is an uncommon event. Aided by good food, warm houses and advanced medicine most children grow to adulthood in Britain today. In the past, however, children died in large numbers. Most went unremarked but occasionally one made the headlines. Such a case occurred in Westleigh in 1911

In October of that year a Mrs Hoard of London travelled by train to the village to leave her grandchild Arthur Hoard with a Mrs Moss who had advertised her services as a 'foster mother' in various publications, charging 7s (35p) per month. Arthur was left with her and Mrs Hoard travelled straight back to London. The next day, however, Mrs Moss found that the child would not, or could not, eat and that it was very ill. She panicked and 'telegraphed to Mrs Hoard to come and take it away.' She also called in Doctor Thompson from Bideford but the child died just three days later.

At the inquest that followed the Coroner denounced Mrs Moss as a 'Baby farmer.' The term has now gone out of use but it refers to the old practice of mothers dumping unwanted – usually illegitimate – children with a 'foster mother.' Once the child was 'out of sight' it was also 'out of mind' and often death soon followed through lack of care or effort on the 'baby farmer's' part. A famous fictional case appears in Chapter Two of *Oliver Twist*. That the child in this case was illegitimate was admitted by a Mr Hoard from Croyde, the grandfather, who said the boy had been born in Battersea Female Mission.

The medical evidence at the case came from a Dr. Pearson who reckoned death was due to malnutrition. The coroner and jury actually visited Moss's house and on returning to court agreed on a verdict of death by misadventure though strongly censuring all concerned. The 'baby farmer's house was unfit' and 'the person was unfit.' The Female Mission authorities were condemned for allowing a baby in their care to be so treated and the mother and grandparents were also strongly censured.

'Baby farmers' are no longer with us thank goodness, but, as recent cases have shown, child abuse still continues though, mercifully, death is a rare event.

North Devon Journal 4.2.1985

TOWN AND LANDSCAPE

19. WHAT BECAME OF THE OLD TOWN CROSS?

Place names are fascinating records of the past. Each name, whether it refers to a town, village, street or field has some meaning be it ever so bizarre or whimsical. One name in Barnstaple, for example, recalls a major feature of the town now long gone.

Cross Street was named after the large cross, probably on a pedestal, that stood at its junction with High Street. This spot of course was opposite the main entrance to the churchyard and thus a good site for such a holy structure. Nobody is quite certain when it was built but there is a reference as early as 1500 to one penny being spent 'to repair the High Cross'. In 1542, fourpence was 'paid for the high Cross light' – though whether this was a holy candle of a proper 'street light' I do not know. Seventeen years later 1s.8d. (9p) was spent by the corporation to repair the stocks at High Cross. Clearly this central location was chosen as a suitable site for criminals to be displayed to public derision.

For some unexplained reason the cross was pulled down in 1560 though its base may have survived. Possibly the old cross had become beyond repair; perhaps it smacked too much of 'popery' for the newly-founded Church of England. Whatever the reason the cross went – but the name stayed.

In 1614, for example, threepence was spent 'for watching flesh hung up to the High Cross in Lent'. This odd payment referred to the church ruling about not eating meat during Lent then in force. Its exposure in public was presumably meant as a warning to others.

Slightly later, in 1631, two men appeared in the town court and admitted fighting at High Cross, whilst during the Civil War shortly afterwards a poor trooper was hung at 'High Cross'.

The last reference to the cross I can find (apart from Cross Street itself) is an advertisement in the *Journal* in 1835 when a J. Marsh, ironmonger, was selling his business 'situate at the Red-Cross in the centre of High Street' The 'Red-Cross' might have been a shop sign but I think it is more likely to have been our old cross site.

It is recorded that the walls and gates of old Barnstaple were built of 'a fine flesh coloured sandstone'. It would appear likely that the cross was of the same material – thus explaining the red name unless

the memory of the hanging or the public exposure of meat was still current! Some of this stone was used in the old Blue Coat school but was covered up in the late nineteenth century.
North Devon Journal 12.1.1989

20. ROADS HAVE NEW NAMES

How well do you know Barnstaple? Many Barumites pride themselves on their knowledge of their home town but place names have changed over the centuries and if we could go back in time all of us would experience problems in asking directions.

It would, for example, be no use asking for Joy Street before the mid-seventeenth century as before that time it was always known as Eastgate Street – a name that first appears in documents from 1430. It seems to have been renamed when the prominent Joye family lived there. A similar but more difficult problem would face us if we asked for Tuly Street. In its earliest form the areas was known as North Hay but began being called after the local St Olaves Well which in time became corrupted to Tooley and then Tuly. Our ancestors were nothing if not inventive.

One of the smallest thoroughfares in Barnstaple is Theatre Lane which links High Street with the Strand. As its name suggests this was the site of the town's theatre but prior to its building around 1870 the narrow way was known as Honeypot Lane.

Another small road that has changed its name is Paiges Lane. Now a 'dog leg' behind Marks and Spencer's it was known by its present title as far back as 1513. At some period it lost this title and became known by the name of a pub there as Elephant Lane. Why the inn was called this is anyone's guess but when the pub disappeared usage of the old name was resumed.

Another 'lost' name was Southgate Street. This referred to the section of High Street from the Square to its junction with Cross Street. Similarly the length of High Street from Holland Walk to Northgate was known as North Street.

Cross Street referred to above is a corruption of Crok Street which legend has it refers to the old pottery industry or retailing that used to be carried on there. Another reminder of an old industry is Anchor Lane which was earlier known as Enker Lane. This latter is an example of how some names have changed little – yet the alteration has been enough to cause mystification today. Bear Street is one such being a corruption of Bar Street. An old writer states that 'Streets of this name are found in nearly all fortified places, leading up to the gate itself.' The road only became Bear Street around 1700.

Another name taken from a disappeared feature is that of Belle Meadow– now a car park off the Square. This area was originally one of gardens owned by the town's rich merchants.

It is possible through a little historical work to locate most of these changelings or vanished routeways but a few still remain mysterious. Among these are Onge Lane and Cuker Lane, both referred to in fourteenth century documents, and what of Ram Alley, Alleins Lane, Bowman's Lane and the intriguing Mount Lugg?

Perhaps it is only fitting to note that some old names have received a new lease of life, the obvious example being Green Lane. Previously a very underused 'short cut' it now graces the first totally enclosed street in Barnstaple and looks set to remain for at least another few centuries.

North Devon Journal 16.4.1992

21. FLAX: THE FIRST CROP TO GAIN FARM SUBSIDY

That 'nothing is new' is an adage – and it even applies to such apparently modern innovations as agricultural subsidies. At the Devon Record Office is a small bundle of papers dating from the years 1782 to 1785 relating to the activities of one William Hole of Barnstaple. He describes himself as 'farmer' and the crop dealt with in these papers was flax.

This plant is today associated mainly with the linen industry in Northern Ireland but at that date it was a vital ingredient in the making of sails for the ships of Britain. In the early 1780s the Government became very worried that most of Britain's flax seemed to be imported from Russia. In 1781, therefore, to ensure a constant supply of this strategic material the Government offered a subsidy of 4d (2p) on every stone (14 lbs) of flax grown.

In South and East Devon quite a few individuals became involved in the plant's production but in North Devon surviving records only mention William Hole. He appears to have been a considerable land owner – either that or he rented small parcels of land to grow his crops on. The documents in the Record Office refer to his claims for the subsidy or bounty as it was then termed.

A typical claim reads 'I William Hole of Barnstaple in the said County of Devon, Farmer of a Tenement called The Long Closes at

Pottington in the parish of Pilton and County aforesaid. By virtue of an Act of Parliament pass'd ye 31st Day of October (1781) Crave leave to claim the Bounty; granted by the said Act to the Growers of Flax, on about Nine Acres of midling Flax, rose on the said Tenement in the Current Year, which will probably produce and yield about 210 Stone of Flax (of 14 lbs to the Stone) when broke and properly prepared and dress'd fit for Market – Witness my hand this 7th Day of October 1782 William Hole.'

Other claims are in respect of 108 stone from 'Stonyard' in Barnstaple, 190 stone from 'Lower Mullycott, Ilfordcombe', 400 stone from 'Pill' in Bishop's Tawton and 230 stone from 'Venton' and 'Higher Uppacott' in Monkleigh. All this flax was produced in the one year of 1782.

Accompanying the claims are dockets indicating where the flax went. William Cayne & Co. of Yeovil, Somerset 'sail cloth makers' acknowledged receipt of nearly 4,000 lbs of flax. Other purchasers included George Privett & Co. of Bristol, Thomas Tucker of Bridport and two Barnstaple flax manufacturers – John Davolls and Robert Lamprey who, however, only purchased 252 lbs between them. Visitors to Bridport can still see the original flax and hemp machinery preserved there in the local museum.

Hole wasn't just the producer but also took some part in the manufacturing process. Flax is a very fibrous plant and must be 'retted' or broken down into its constituent strands and this is done by rotting it in pits from 10 days to a fortnight. Hole was careful to note that all his flax was 'by me broken and properly prepared for market.'

It must have been a lucrative crop as the price in 1808 was £11 16s 3d (£11.81) an acre and William grew 54 acres in 1782 – a net income of £637.74 not forgetting the 'bounty' which amounted to an extra £19.

Not an excessive sum it is true but worth claiming. Both the subsidy and indeed the whole industry have now gone – but the precedent set still remains – an intriguing case of continuity.

North Devon Journal 4.12.1986

22. 'A TOWN SO RICH SO GOOD, SO...'

Poets are used to abuse. Work that was once liked is now despised and vice versa. Most criticism is usually well-deserved and perhaps none more so than that directed at the Rev. Richard Taprelll a local clergyman who broke into print in 1806 with his 115 page poem entitled simply *Barnstaple*.

Sixty years later J. R. Chanter in his *Literary History of Barnstaple* wrote that the poem 'was written in such an absurd and stilted style as really to be a burlesque.' He adds a further damnation that much of it is 'certainly very amusing for its very absurdity.'

Chanter's remarks are all too true concerning the literary merit of the work but even he had to admit that the poem is still of some interest in recalling how the town once appeared. The poem is based on the idea of a few friends walking round the town street by street describing what they see. From this they would 'draw such moral, religious, entertaining and improving reflections from the whole, as such a variety is in its own nature calculated to suggest' as the author put it.

Taprell begins at Litchdon Street, then the main entrance to the town, which is dismissed as

> 'An entrance too rough and
> Dirty dost that furnish to a Town so
> Rich, so good, so large, so full of fame as
> BARNSTAPLE.'

After Litchdon Street the poet arrives at the Square – then railed in against cattle. Apparently it wasn't very attractive in the early 1800s only becoming beautiful when, 'BARUM's fair inhabitants enter it.'

From here Taprell moved to the High Street where he used a good many lines to describe the church, its monuments and the churchyard which he called 'this hill of human dust.' The quietness of this scene gave way to the bustle of the well-stocked market although he notes,

> 'How trying to the Poor who
> All this rich provision see and hardly
> Gain a taste.'

Walking onwards the poet reached North Walk, 'the boast of BARNSTAPLE'. This curving walk with its many trees was especially attractive in sunlight when many strollers in the height of fashion 'adorn this WALK of Elegance and Beauty.'

The walk was also open to the poor and Taprell has a lovely piece urging them not to feel jealous of the well-fed rich. No doubt it eased their hunger to know that.

> 'Of the heavy cares and
> Mental distresses which your Superiors
> Are condemn'd to feel, ignorant are you.'

It's hard being rich! North Walk is now covered by the Civic Centre and its car parks.

The poet then passes to the Castle with the grand house of the owner next to it (removed within the last 10 years). He climbs the Castle mound and sees the Taw,

> 'Like one broad, vast and immense plate or sheet
> Of SILVER to dazzled eyes looks certain.'

Continuing along he reached Pilton Bridge where there was:

> 'The ship-builder's yard and the
> Large wide-spreading venerable Trees near.'

At this point Taprell even managed to write thirty lines or so on the drowning of three boys who had gone swimming in the Yeo. He follows this, somewhat oddly, with a section on a 'great defect' – ie the absence of a Sunday school in Barnstaple.

The poem concludes with a long section praising in very flattering terms the local landed gentry – possibly to help sell more copies of his poem? It cost two shillings and sixpence ($12\frac{1}{2}$ p) – roughly a third of a working man's weekly wage at that date.

Any one reading *Barnstaple* can only agree with J. R. Chanter when he labels it 'this strange production.' One wonders what Taprell's contemporaries made of it all?

North Devon Journal 3.1.1988

23. PREDICTING THE TOWN'S FUTURE!

Many newspaper readers, if asked, admit to turning to the letters page first. If human nature is as unchanging as I believe it to be then our ancestors probably did so as well.

In September 1831, readers of the *Journal* would have seen a letter from a correspondent signing himself 'BY' addressing itself to the development of Ilfracombe. 'BY' claimed to be a frequent visitor and felt 'a sincere interest in its prosperity' – so much so that he (or she) was moved to suggest 'a few additions to the many improvements that have been already effected with such manifest advantage to the town.'

The writer's first idea concerned the establishment of 'regular steam communication' by sea between Ilfracombe and Bristol, to be supplemented with a new road to Barnstaple. These would render 'this remote but attractive spot' easily accessible and 'enhance the value of property in the town and neighbourhood.'

A second suggestion was that 'better accommodation than exists at present for enjoying the luxury and benefit of bathing' be provided. Apparently the previous two years had seen 'a couple of machines in attendance.' These would have been the cumbersome wheeled huts where shy Georgians could change and from which they could enter the sea away from prying eyes. The year 1831, however, had seen only 'one solitary and sorry machine' in operation. This meant 'fair damsels on the beach at Wildersmouth' had to wait several hours to bathe.

Clearly bathing was a bee in 'BY's' bonnet as he went on to suggest that 'the rocks at Wildersmouth might be easily blasted and levelled, to admit three or four machines being used at the same time, which might be drawn up and done by means of a windlass or two.' A further refinement would be the erection of a few tents which could provide much better shelter and greater privacy than the rocks which the women 'are now obliged to resort for lack of other accommodation.'

'BY's' last suggestion followed his noticing that many of the 'back walks' around Ilfracombe were disfigured with small pools of 'stagnant water' and heaps of rubbish and decayed vegetable. In addition many of the drains were still above ground and were no better than open sewers, especially one the length of the 'main street' 'BY' suggested they be buried which would help the appearance of the town no end.

Whoever 'BY' was the suggestions were sensible and, as Ilfracombe's later development as a major seaside resort showed, clearly a prediction of some foresight.

North Devon Journal 4.1.1990

24. FIRE CAN BE THE GREATEST ENEMY LEAST EXPECTED

Nowadays the dreaded cry of 'fire' generally leads to a telephone call to the nearest fire station and the rapid arrival of a modern fully-equipped fire engine. In the past, however, when our ancestors lived in wood and thatch houses, fire was an ever present enemy especially as contemporary fire engines were primitive.

In April 1832 a particularly serious blaze hit one part of Barnstaple. The first alarm was raised at 3am on a Sunday morning when 'the inhabitants of this town were aroused from their peaceful slumbers by the oft repeated cry of fire and the clashing of the parish bells.'

The cause of all the alarm was the discovery of smoke and flames coming from the newly-built shop of Mr Stribling, a cabinet maker, at the Northgate in High Street. The shop was full of inflammable substances and the fire had got such a hold that it 'excited the most alarming apprehensions for the safety of the whole of that part of the town' as a local journalist put it.

The ringing of the bells, however, had brought the fire engine crew out. Their engine was basically a hand-operated pump, probably like the engine preserved today in South Molton museum. The only injury was to a young boy, probably an apprentice, who slept on the premises. He 'did not awake until his bed was on fire', when his only means on escape was via a high window. He leapt out and was 'seriously hurt' but apparently soon recovered.

The situation was made worse by a high wind which continually carried sparks to the roofs of nearby buildings but these were 'speedily extinguished by the application of a powerful stream of water from the engines.'

The *Journal*, in reporting the conflagration noted that Mr Stribling 'a persevering and industrious tradesman' only had about a quarter of the destroyed goods insured. In addition most of his workmen had lost their 'expensive tools' in the fire and thus faced unemployment if not total ruin.

What happened to the unfortunate workers I do not know but reference to *Pigot and Co's Royal National and Commercial Directory* for 1844 shows the presence of William Stribling as a carpenter and joiner at 50 High Street, so apparently the fire didn't destroy him for good. Indeed, in later directories, William is shown as having branched out into upholstery as well and his business continued until at least 1870.

One suspects that he was more careful about fire and insurance!
North Devon Journal 15.3.1990

25. THE DEMISE OF LIMEKILNS

In the recently published book *Out of the World and into Combe Martin* one of the chapters deals with the limekilns of the village and how important they were to the local economy. Limestone was both quarried locally and imported to feed the limekilns, the resulting material being used by farmers all over North Devon to 'sweeten' their land and to increase output. The authors deal at some length with the trade but did not point out the paucity of records before 1850.

Recently I same across a long letter in the *Journal* dated January 30 1840, which supplies a lot more details. The author was shy of publicity, just signing himself 'A reviewer of the lime trade of Combmartin.'

He began, 'It is a fact obvious to all the inhabitants of Combmartin that the lime trade is the principal support of the place.' Indeed, he continued 'the greatest part of the peasantry derive their subsistence by labouring in the limestone quarries.'

Apparently income from the trade fluctuated fairly sharply. In the period 1810-20 income was high and the business 'was in a very flourishing state.' From 1820 to 1840, however, profits all but disappeared and many limeburners abandoned their kilns. The writer then posed the question – what caused this downturn?

He proceeded to try and answer it by dismissing the influence of coal and labour prices. In fact over the years in question they had actually fallen. No, the reason for the decline was due to the absence of a regulated and recognised measure of lime. Because of this the lime merchants were losing between a sixth and an eighth of the income they should have been receiving.

This came about because of the way in which the trade was organised. A landowner would agree with a merchant to let his land for quarrying at so much a bushel of lime extracted. Owing to the lack of a standard measure the bigger it was the more profit he made.

Not only the owners lost out. From about 1839 on a new system had been introduced whereby quarries were leased 'by the job.' The merchant would contract with a gang of six to eight men to work for a year at agreed rates of 80p to £1.20 a bushel. As he made sure these bushels were as large as possible the actual workers naturally got less for their labour.

The corrupt system, however, didn't benefit the lime merchants as local farmers also expected generous measures of lime when they bought in supplies – so the only losers were the local people of Combe Martin whatever their position in the trade. The letter ended with a plea for a reform of the system.

The writer advised that 'the lime mercants of Combmartin, and the neighbouring parishes...be convened together, and to embrace the first opportunitiy to consider the most effectual means to prevent the recurrence of these evils.'

One assumes that the locals took heed of this as the limeburning trade continued in the village until just before the Second World War. By then it wasn't sharp practices that killed the trade, rather the development of artificial fertilisers cheap enough to be used by all which finally closed the quarries.

North Devon Journal 12.9.1991

26. SHEDDING LIGHT ON AN OUTCRY

Readers of the *Journal* are well-served by reports of local council meetings, which, it must be said, are usually decorous and well-ordered. In November 1841, however, the *Journal* reported on a meeting at Ilfracombe that was 'one of the most uproarious of the usually uproarious meetings of this parish.'

The event was the annual vestry meeting. Ilfracombe at this date had no actual council but was run by a group of rich local men who had originally met in the church vestry hence the name. Few people, then or now, liked paying rates and this particular meeting had been called to discuss a motion to stop lighting the town in order to save money.

On the appointed day 'a large number of the most respectable inhabitants' assembled at the market house and heard a Mr Stabb stress the importance of Ilfracombe 'keeping pace with the country generally in the march of convenience and civilisation.' He asked his fellow townsmen to support his motion to keep the gaslights in the town lit and paid for out of the rates.

The vote was taken and the motion was passed and the meeting moved on to appoint two lighting inspectors. Defeated in their attempts to save money the anti-lighters put up their own candidates – a move which led to 'a loud and vehement altercation.' Indeed the row 'exceeded anything that has hitherto taken place at the generally boisterous meetings in this town' and a 'general skrimmage' took place at the back of the hall. When the vote was eventually taken the pro-light candidates won.

The next step was to set the rates in the knowledge that the sum of £135 was required to keep alight the 32 lamps in the town. One of the antis, Mr Dennis, observed that the Ilfracombe lights cost £3 each per year to run while those in Barnstaple cost only £2. He reckoned the difference was due to 'collusion' between the lighting inspectors and the directors of the Ilfracombe Gas Company and he proposed a lighting rate of only £80.

At this point a Mr Parry, a director of the maligned Gas Company pointed out that his fellow directors had made very little profit and had only ever paid out one dividend in its four years of existence – and then only of four per cent which was hardly profiteering.

He was followed by a Mr Bligh who reckoned that the claim by the anti-lighters to be 'friends of the poor' was hypocritical as the poor paid little towards the rates anyway. If the antis really wanted to support the poor would they join with him in voluntarily doubling their own rates rates contributions? A deafening silence was the answer. A Mr Jones then pointed out that rates per head had actually fallen over the last 20 years because of the recent building boom in the town which brought more ratepayers in.

Come the vote the pro-lighters won easily – especially as an unusually large group of ladies (ratepayers in their own right) had turned out to add their vote to those for the lights.

As the *Journal* report concluded, 'the excitement of the town the occasion was only equalled, in degree, by the exultation of all the respectable inhabitants at the defeat of the attempt to place them in darkness.'

North Devon Journal 20.4.1992

27. HOW BANKING CAME TO THE HIGH STREET

One of the constant complaints today is that our town centres are being swamped by banks, estate agents and building societies – the three types of business now apparently becoming indistinguishable.

Only 200 years ago, however, there were no banks in North Devon.

The first was established in 1791 at Barnstaple and went under the name of Cutcliffe, Roche, Gribble and Company, although it soon became known as 'The Old Bank.' It was based in a house opposite the Market in High Street, the site of which is now apparently occupied by Stephens' Bakery.

The three men who started the business were all well known and well placed in the community. C. N. Cutcliffe, of Marwood Hill, was a member of 'an old and wealthy Devonshire family.' Monier Roche, as the name suggests, was of French descent via a Huguenot family who came to North Devon.

His family name was Anglicised to Rock and one of his descendants gave Rock Park to the town. He was described as 'a moneyed man, in extensive business as a merchant, with shrewdness and commercial ability.'

The third member of the company and junior partner was W. Gribble, a solicitor.

The three men – gentleman, merchant and lawyer – provided a firm base for the new bank which, if we believe a report of 1871, 'maintained a reputation for honour and stability rivalled by that of few private banking firms anywhere.' This reference to 'stability' strikes us as odd today but all through the 19th century private banks were going into liquidation, taking investors' money with them.

Within a few years both Cutcliffe and Roche had died and been replaced by Zachary Drake 'a country gentleman of very old family.' As 'Drake and Gribble' the bank continued until Gribble died and was replaced by his son Henry, who also soon died and was replaced by William who, in turn, was quickly replaced by a John Gribble in 1809.

The firm remained as a two-partner company for 20 years and built up its connections and deposits as local farmers came to trust its financial stability. At the time John joined the firm it had a competitor in the shape of the 'North Devon Bank.' By this date, however, Barnstaple had developed sufficiently to support two banks and the two continued in friendly rivalry.

'The Old Bank', however, seems to have had the better manager, if we are to judge from the contemporary description of John Gribble with his 'faultless integrity of his personal character, his strong sense and the severe plainness of his manner of life,' which 'combined to give him a degree of influence in which he was entirely unapproached

41

by any townsman of his time.'

In 1830 John Marshall joined the bank and it became Drake, Gribble, Marshall and Company (no wonder most people called it The Old Bank!). In 1846 Gribble died and was replaced by Henry Gribble who died in 1866 'at his desk.' The family nature of these early banks is shown by the fact that this Henry had married the daughter of the bank's chief clerk. Similarly when Mr Marshall died he was succeeded by his nephew who in turn was replaced by his son.

So, it went on until 1887 by which time it had become Marshall, Harding, Hiern and Company. In this year the company was taken over by Messrs Fox, Fowler and Company. The change was apparently very sudden and 'some little uneasiness was felt and disquieting rumour got abroad' in the town but were soon quelled as the bank ran normally, although from different premises.

These were situated in Cross Street and now house Lloyd's Bank – who acquired them after taking over Fox, Fowler and Company in 1921.

The Old Bank's competitor, the North Devon Bank, was taken over by National Provincial in 1835 and this bank survived in its building at the top of Cross Street until itself being amalgamated to form the National Westminster.

North Devon Journal-Herald 31.7.1986

28. ILFRACOMBE GETS ITS FIRST CLEAN-UP

Ilfracombe has always had a reputation as a healthy town, indeed its nineteenth century growth was based on its good name as a 'watering place.' In November 1849, however, after an outbreak of cholera, a three day visit by a Government health inspector revealed a very different picture.

The inspector invited locals to give evidence and the first was a Mr Vye who reckoned the town to be in a 'very filthy condition' as the town's waste was merely thrown into the 'mill stream' and ended up in the harbour or spread about the lower lying part of Ilfracombe. A Mr Turner added to this by pointing out that in summer the water level went down so much that the stream dried up and he didn't have enough water to flush his toilet.

Turner went on to complain about the local churchyard where the last burial only a few days before 'was laid within six inches from the surface' as it was so full and no alternative was available. In addition, cracks in the pavement of the church 'permitted the most odious escapes from the vaults underneath.'

Local architect Lewis Butcher gave evidence on the sewerage system of the town admitting that he had seen 'night soil, ie human faeces, lying in the open gutters' which had overflown from the cesspits. He then gave some shocking figures. In Water Street there wasn't a single toilet in any of the houses. In another area there were 70 houses with 300 inhabitants sharing just seven toilets! Rather obviously one would have thought, he added that 'the smells in all parts of the town were often most offensive.'

He was followed by a whole succession of witnesses who added horror on horror as they described in nauseating detail further examples of careless sewage disposal at Hillsborough and Montpellier Terraces. In the latter case, the sewerage pipe merely carried the waste matter to a field opposite where it emptied behind a wall.

The result of all this evidence was a complete overhaul of the town's drains and water pipes which, although it cost a large sum, was clearly and urgently needed. The fact that Ilfracombe continued to flourish as a resort town for the next century is clear evidence of the value of this 'clean up'.

North Devon Journal 16.11.1989

29. HISTORIC RITE OF FALLING INTO STREAMS

Many old customs, both good and bad, have passed away with our ancestors. One of the better ones we might well resuscitate is 'beating the bounds.' Simply explained this was the walking of the parish boundaries by a group of local people who stopped at major land marks and 'beat' a boy to ensure he remembered where the boundary ran! In some places they were less aggressive and allowed the boys to 'beat' the boundary marks with a willow wand. At Barnstaple the earliest record we have of the ceremony is from 1484, though it is almost certain it was being performed long before this. One full description of the ceremony is in the *North Devon Journal* which reported at great length the events of June 30 1891.

The 'beating' party was made up of boys from the nine schools then in the town (both private and public), teachers, clergy, mayor Richard Lake and councillors, the borough accountant, foreman of works, inspector of nuisances, mace-bearers, three policemen, several reporters, two county councillors, numerous members of the public and two 'old inhabitants,' – Mr Gabriel (73) and George Jones (70) who had beaten the bounds years before.

The party numbered more than 100 and they set off in drizzle in procession along the High Street. The weather, however, was on their side and it had brightened by the time they reached Rolle Bridge.

At East Pilton Marsh field – now Pottington – they had to climb a five-bar gate and cross some fields to Poles Hill Lane, now widened, but then 'a true Devonshire lane', wide enough only for two men walking abreast. Where it met Hall's Mill Lane at the bottom of Upcott Hill they stopped for their first rest.

At this point there was some dispute over the true boundary but it was settled by Mr Gabriel's memory of his previous 'beating'. One boy in the group then managed to fall in to Bradiford Water so no doubt he remembered the boundary too!

On went the party to Shearford Lane when 'mud of the thickest Devonshire type was encountered.' This lane was reckoned to be 'one of the most ancient thoroughfares of the locality,' having been hollowed out of solid rock to a depth of 12 feet.

Trudging up Roborough the party began to lose some of its members but the hardier kept going along mysteriously named Smoky House Lane (still there today) down to the Yeo. Here the river had to be crossed twice 'with the inevitable result that the fun became fast and furious.' Planks were used to make a narrow bridge and not unexpectedly one of the party fell in.

After pulling him out the 'beaters' continued to follow the boundary along the Yeo, through lush meadows until they reached Ivy Lodge, the gatehouse to the 'big house' known as Stoneyard where the Incledon family lived. When first built this had apparently been 'the best example of a castellated mansion in the kingdom, the completeness of the scheme of the owner extending even to the plate and the earthenware, the decorative designs upon which were of a piece with the splendid structure itself.'

The owner later demolished the house leaving only a dairy building standing. It was at the Lodge that the party stopped for lunch – at the Mayor's expense.

'When creature comforts had been restored' the walk continued 'at a swinging pace' via Little Lilly Lane to Maidenford where they crossed a stream via a bridge that 'stood in three parishes.' Leaving the road the party walked alongside the stream towards Newport but Beadle Hancock lost his footing and fell into the stream though he manfully kept the mace above his head as he went under.

The group halted whilst the wet Beadle regained his dignity and the Mayor initiated a series of races with pennies as prizes. Sprinting and 'wheelbarrow racing' went down well and were followed by the 'Corporation Handicap' of 200 yards. This was won, rather surprisingly considering he weighed 14 stone, by the Mayor 'with a good turn of speed,' whilst an under 30s race was won by the Mayor's son Bruce Lake.

After these jollities the party moved off again hugging the banks of the stream still today known as Coney Gut. In the thirteenth-century this had been called South Eaux or South Water – to match the North Eaux (later the Yeo) to the North. The going here was fairly easy and the reporter noted 'The rapid march of the borough officials through thicket, meadow and ditch to the Devon and Somerset railway' (now dismantled) in Whiddon Valley.

From here they made their way from Mount Sandford Road near the old Convent School up Windy Ash Hill at the back of Rumsam and along a brook called Wood-street-water. It was whilst here that the party ran into trouble. Local farmer John Smith had vowed that no-one would trespass on his land and had stationed himself in one of his fields carrying a club in one hand and a notice threatening prosecution to anyone who trespassed.

As the 'beaters' came into sight he defied them to come any further and indeed hit the leader – Town Clerk Bosson – on the shoulder. This was a mistake as this august official didn't stand on his dignity but merely knocked Mr Smith down who was then trampled underfoot by the rest of the party! Getting to his feet after the crowd had passed he roared for his gun but it was too late – the 'beaters' had gone.

Reaching the Taw a small flotilla of boats 'flying gay pennons' took the party down to the Long bridge. The boats sailed on to the railway bridge behind where the present-day Civic Centre now stands, and up the Yeo. At this point the Foreman of Works fell in to the river – apparently pushed by one of the other passengers!

A pleasing, if somewhat tiring, ceremony and one that has sadly been let die in recent years. Indeed the last record I have of 'beating the bounds' around Barnstaple is from 1909. Has it occurred more recently? Perhaps I could make the suggestion that it is revived soon – and not just for Barnstaple but for all the towns and parishes of North Devon. Who will be the first to take up the challenge?

North Devon Journal 10.9.1987

30. REMEMBERED IN BRONZE

Barnstaple Square is crossed by thousands of people every day yet how many people have ever noticed or inspected the bronze bust standing on the grassed island in the middle? The statue commemorates one of the town's greatest men of the Victorian age – Charles Sweet Willshire.

His name is unknown to most today yet at his death in 1889 the *Journal* reckoned that he was 'better known than any other man in North Devon.' He was in fact one of those figures from the last century who seem larger than life to us today. Who then was he?

He was born in 1837, the son of Thomas Willshire, who had come to Barnstaple around 1830 and established an iron foundry in Newport from where he turned out agricultural implements and household ironmongery. His son went to school in the town and on leaving entered the family business inheriting the company in time and building it up to one of the largest concerns in North Devon.

From before he was 21, however, Charles was taking an interest in local politics and soon after 'coming of age' he was elected on to the town council as one of its youngest members. He continued to be re-elected for the next 30 years being made an alderman and serving as mayor twice.

Whilst on the council he also served as a local magistrate though it was common knowledge that 'he many times paid fines imposed by himself so the delinquent who was unable to pay should not go to prison.'

He was director of many public bodies, involved with several local Friendly Societies as well as being a Guardian of the Poor i.e. an official who helped distribute poor relief.

In addition he was a major in the local Volunteers (forerunners of the Territorial Army) and a one-time master of the Barnstaple Freemasons.

He died aged just 53 after a life devoted to the people and town of his birth. His widow, whom he married in 1860, was the daughter of Lord Fortescue's steward, but they had no children. His death was so lamented that wellwishers from across the whole political spectrum subscribed to his memorial bust which was made by the well-known local artist Baron.

At its unveiling in August 1892, the whole council plus police and two companies of Volunteers, collected in the Square to pay tribute to Willshire. The Square itself owed its present form to Willshire, who had it laid out during his mayoralty.

Memories, however, are only as long as the oldest person who remembers, and Willshire is now all but forgotten – his bust, now marooned on a traffic island, his only link with today.

North Devon Journal 14.3.1991

30. WEATHER WREAKS HAVOC

The greenhouse effect we are told, will lead to increased flooding in low-lying areas of the world. North Devon is no stranger to floods, one of the worst experienced being in 1894. After an unusually wet year some 3.5 inches of rain fell almost solidly over three days in November which led to tremendous damage all over North Devon and the West of England in general.

Worst struck was Braunton where the River Caen burst burst its banks and flooded the local school and all of Caen Street to a depth of three feet damaging stock in the shops and furniture in the houses. The railway station was cut off and could only be reached by boat. On a sadder note a boy called Corney was playing on the bridge just outside the station when he fell into the river and was swept away to his death.

At Bishop's Tawton the Taw overflowed across the low-lying valley and left some cottages completely cut off. In one lived an old lady, Mrs Sampson and her daughter. They had gone to bed early and were oblivious of the worsening danger but one of their neighbours having seen some seven feet of water swirling around the cottage collected a rescue party.

They weren't a minute too soon as on arriving at the site the cottage began to collapse. Using a long ladder they climbed on to the roof and took out the women via a large hole just before the cob-built cottage disintegrated completely.

Elsewhere in North Devon the floods wreaked havoc. Large areas in Bideford were flooded and the whole of the Kenwith valley was under water while Weare Giffard was 'almost submerged.' Indeed in this village many people had to be rescued from upper windows by requisitioned punts.

Further up the Torridge at Torrington the Stevenstone Hunt kennels were flooded and many hounds drowned though the horses were saved. A stretch of the Marland Light Railway was washed away disrupting the clay works badly.

At Landkey large numbers of livestock were lost and many houses had four inches of water in their ground floor while at Barnstaple the whole of Rock Park, the Square and the area around Whiddon Valley were flooded. As it went under Barnstaple Bridge sightseers saw 'large quantities of hurdles, trees, marigolds, turnips and occasionally the carcass of a sheep' pass underneath.

The rain that gave rise to all this damage eventually ceased and the great clearing-up operation began although many hayricks and cottage gardens had been totally devastated along with buildings and river banks. The 1894 storm was long talked of as the 'worst disaster in living memory.' Let us hope we never see anything so bad.

North Devon Journal 5.9.1991

32. CARVING OUT A LANDMARK

At the eastern end of Bideford's Long Bridge are a pair of small gardens. In one is a slender pedestal topped by a bust of J. Pine-Coffin. Vandalised some time ago it has been cleaned up and is now very attractive again. But who was the subject of the statue?

John Richard Pine-Coffin came from a very ancient family settled for many years at Portledge, just outside Bideford. In the manner of his class John lived quietly on his estate but 'rose at the call of duty to a sense of the responsibility attaching to his position' as a contemporary put it. This 'duty' consisted of acting as a local magistrate, a 'Guardian of the Poor' (the equivalent of our Social Security Officers) and a Conservative County Councillor.

When he died very suddenly aged just 48 in 1890 a local committee was established to raise a subscription list in order to have the bust prepared. At the time it was suggested that this was a Tory response to the erection of a bust to a Liberal politician in Barnstaple Square – an event I covered in an earlier article.

The money needed was quickly raised and a Mr Williamson of Esher, Surrey was commissioned to carve the likeness in white Sicilian marble from a photograph of the deceased.

Unfortunately a snag arose over where the finished product should (or could) be placed. It took a year's wrangling before the Bridge Trust finally agreed to have it in their Bridge-end garden. Here it was finally erected and unveiled at a well attended ceremony in September 1894.

Lord Clinton gave the main speech praising his late friend and ending with the hope 'That the youth of Bideford and neighbourhood, when they looked on this memorial would remember that it was a memorial to a good and upright English gentleman who tried to do his duty.' This slightly ambiguous sentiment met with 'loud cheers.' Lord Clinton then removed the covering sheet and added a well-known landmark to the Bideford scene.

The garden in which it rests is now in the ownership of the nearby Royal Hotel but recently the town council paid for the cleaning of the statue. Interestingly it is said that in 1943 the mayor of the day took his scrubbing brush to the bust to clean it up. It was noted at the time that the job should be carried out again in 1993 by the then mayor – an interesting anniversary to look forward to perhaps?

North Devon Journal 29.8.1991

33. 'VANDALISM' IS CERTAINLY NOTHING NEW

It seems that hardly a week passes when the *Journal* doesn't contain reports of mindless vandalism having occurred somewhere in North Devon. Many people will blame the age we live in and will, perhaps, look back to a rosy 'golden age' when vandals were unknown.

It comes as a rude shock therefore to turn to the newspapers of March 1912 and find the headline 'Dastardly acts at Barnstaple – many shop windows damaged.' The story that followed rivals anything we read of today.

During one night 'many of the plate glass windows of the tradespeople's establishments had been subjected to the most wanton damage by means of glass cutting and other instruments.' Virtually all the shops in High Street and Joy Street had been attacked along with several in Boutport Street – altogether nearly a hundred windows were damaged.

Glaziers called in to replace the glass were of the opinion that a wheel-cutting machine had been used and ruled out the use of a diamond ring. Whoever did it had made long cuts across the windows except in one or two cases where a series of shorter cuts had been made. The window of Percival Harris, a High Street stationer, had a hole 'about the size of a large pea' which the police put down to an airgun shot.

In collecting evidence, the police were told by R. Charley, a

Boutport Street butcher and Mr Parking, a tailor who lived next door, that their windows had been attacked some three weeks previously in the same manner. From this the somewhat obvious deduction was drawn 'that the offender or offenders have been at work some time.'

Needless to say the 'outrages...caused the greatest...indignation among the townspeople.' The police were 'making the most careful enquiries into the matter' but a week later had made no real headway. Indeed they were reduced to offering a £5 reward for any information.

A search of later papers has revealed no arrests in the case and whoever it was appears to have escaped punishment. Next time you read about modern vandalism in North Devon don't automatically assume that it is a modern disease – all communities seem to have suffered from it at all times.

North Devon Journal 5.5.1988

34. HOW MEMORIES OF A MAJOR FIRE NEVER FADE

Major fires tend to stick in people's memories – and none more so in Bideford then the one which destroyed the Old Town School in January 1926. This is still recalled clearly by older residents today and no wonder when one considers how major a conflagration it was.

The school, which accommodated 440 children was heated by nine open fires and one of these must have been the source of the fire, although this point was never proved. Whatever its cause, the flames were first noticed around 11 am by the 'beat constable' P.C. Trim and a Mr C. Tallin who lived opposite the school. The fire alarm was raised and within fifteen minutes the fire engine and its volunteer crew were on the scene.

Whilst waiting for the brigade P.C. Trim had organinsed a human chain from the crowd of onlookers which soon gathered to remove as much furniture as possible from the school.

The firemen, under Captain Morris, quickly got four hoses playing on the flames but were defeated by a strong south westerly wind which fanned the fire to incandescence. Indeed the 'air was thick with smoke and sparks' and a contemporary journalist noted that it was lucky the school was bordered on three sides by the old cemetery 'and so was at a distance from surrounding house properties.'

So fierce was the blaze that the firemen gave up trying to defeat it and merely tried to contain it. They eventually brought the fire under control by 1.30 pm – some three hours after the initial outbreak.

The morning revealed a scene of devastation with only one wing of the old building still standing. Not only had the building been destroyed but all the school registers back to 1860 had been lost along with the whole collection of silver trophies won over the years. Various paintings of former masters plus photographs of 300 old school boys who had fought in the First World War had also been destroyed. In all, the damage was estimated at £4,000. The building itself was insured, but not the furniture inside it.

Life, however, had to go on and at a special meeting the next day the managers arranged to house their pupils at the nearby Geneva School until a new school building could be provided. One oddity is worth noting however – the site of the Old Town School is now occupied by the Bideford Fire Station – a very fitting use!

North Devon Journal 24.5.1990

OCCUPATIONS

35. WHEN MPs COULD BE DISHONEST

Britain is often referred to as the home of Parliamentary style democracy. But just how old this type of government is can be seen when we look at the MPs returned from Barnstaple.

The first we have any record of is one Durand the Cordwainer (shoemaker). He was a local councillor who went up to Westminster in 1295, some 700 years ago. At that date the town was important enough to return two members and he was accompanied by William of Barnstaple. Notice that neither man had a surname, such additions only becoming common in the following century. One wonders how the populace distinguished each other. One way is shown by the next MP who was returned in 1298 and bore the name Philip Bodeport. It has been suggested that his name was taken from where he lived – Boutport Street. Other locationally named MPs followed...Matthew of Chivenor, Walter of Flitton (North Molton), Simon of Brayleigh (East Buckland) and John of Marwood.

The beginning of the fourteenth century saw the start of Barnard de la Bow's parliamentary career for the town. He was returned on no less than seven occasions, the last time being in 1339. Not only was he mayor of the town and a long serving MP but in 1314 he took holy orders – a busy man indeed.

Such long terms in office appear to have been nothing unusual. Thomas de la Barre, first elected in 1325, served in six parliaments.

We know little of these early MPs, so it comes as more of a shock to read how in 1332 Geoffrey of Flitton, the serving MP at that date, was charged with burglary of St Magdalene's Priory in Barnstaple! He was acquitted and went on to be returned four times. Interestingly enough, another man charged with the same burglary became MP in 1338 so clearly robbing church property didn't count too much against one.

Criminality wasn't just a one-way thing with these MPs. In 1360 Walter Phipp was the member for Barnstaple when he was attacked by a murderer. Luckily, he escaped death but one wonders what brought the attack on.

Twenty-five years later John Henrys somehow got into office 'without the knowledge or assent of the Bailiffs or Barnstaple'. The townspeople refused to pay his parliamentary expenses but still couldn't get rid of him. These last few were nothing if not colourful though, of course, many others were dull.

One thing that tended to promote bizarreness was the extremely small size of the electorate. When the vote was confined to just a few prominent townspeople the would-be MP had little need to be popular or even apparently honest. With a few well-placed 'presents' you were in. Indeed, in later centuries Barnstaple and bribery became synonymous, a topic I hope to deal with at a later date.

North Devon Journal 6.7.1989

36. HORSE TRADING 17th CENTURY FASHION

A century ago the horse ruled supreme in North Devon...transport, agriculture and business depended on it. Breeding and selling were of major importance and Barnstaple still provided an annual market for buyers and sellers, traditionally held on the Strand opposite the present bus station. The origins of this market are lost in time but detailed records date from as long ago as 1628. There is still in existence a series of 'Registers of Horses sold at Fairs' covering 1628 to 1652 The sale was generally held on September 8 and these records were kept as a form of insurance – both against the sale of stolen horses and, more obviously, to ensure that taxes due on such sales were paid. The 'tax' or toll for every horse sold was 8d (3p) with smaller tolls on other animals.

The entries are to a standard form and give vendors' and purchasers' names and addresses, prices paid and a note as to any distinguishing features of the animals. The name of a witness is also given in many cases. A typical entry reads 'John Cocke of braunton sold unto Arthur Holmore of Great Torrington one white nagge with a hitch upon the farther eare, price £2 8sh. Anthony Bery of Braunton knoweth the seller.'

To the local historian these fairly 'dry' financial records are of some interest. Firstly we get some idea of prices. Sums changing hands were ridiculously small by our standards but relatively large for that time. An average price of beween £2 and £4 per horse was a hefty sum. The highest recorded price was £8 16s 8d (£8.84) and the lowest just 4s 8d (24p) – one wonders what the poor horse looked like!

Of more interest, perhaps are the addresses. Most people listed are, of course, local but occasionally there is a surprise. There was

Ellis Frye, of Milverton, accompanied by fellow traders from Bristol and Cheddar. Others came from London and South Wales but the most travelled was Arthure Serjante of 'Kirchbe' (Kirkby) in Lancashire who sold a grey gelding for £3 2s 6d (£3.12½) to an Ilfracombe man. Perhaps he was a regular visitor as it is noted that 'The parties knew each other.'

The spelling of most place-names is phonetic and some odd ones occur. Would you recognise Somebridge (Swimbridge), Weare Jefferd (Weare Giffard), Wemory (Wembworthy), Rattenford (Rackenford), Shagford (Chagford) and Shepbeare (Shebbear)? Say them aloud and you will here the authentic seventeenth-century dialect.

Another point of interest is how the horses were individually identified. Most appear to have had an ear mutilated by cutting or slitting. Thus we read of a mare 'top cutt in the neare ear' and another with 'a half penny (mark) in the farther eare.' Branding wasn't as common but does appear occasionally. Thus William Mare's 'nagge' was branded in the 'farther buttocke with a horsehoe' and Robert Bowden's mare bore the letters 'RB'.

The market virtually disappeared during the Civil War years of the 1640s but rapidly re-established itself after this. On average 38 horses were sold each year and the numbers appear to have gradually increased until the growth of the railway sounded the first death knell of the horses' monopoly on transport.

With the introduction of cars in the twentieth-century the Barnstaple horse market withered and died – a sad end to a long history but one that was inevitable.

North Devon Journal 25.7.1985

37. HOLIDAY TRAGEDY AT LYNTON

The full history of tourism in North Devon has yet to be written though it is clear that the industry was well developed by the beginning of the nineteenth century.

A sad story from 1836 sheds some light on how the Georgians spent their holidays. In August of that year Miss Mary Ann Webster, described as a 'maiden lady, between forty and fifty years of age', left Birmingham to holiday in Lynton with her niece and sister.

She came to sample "the romantic and peculiar beauties" of the village and these included a trip to Watersmeet. The rest of the party decided to walk but Miss Webster took a donkey with an eight-year old boy as her guide.

The tourists made their way along the narrow path and Miss Webster was some way ahead of the others when her donkey lost its footing and slipped. This threw the rider who, with great presence of mind, seized the saddle bow to hang suspended over a sixty foot drop. The boy grabbed the animal's bridle to stop it slipping over altogether and both shouted for help. Unfortunately before rescue came the woman's strength gave out and she let go and rolled down into the River Lyn.

The other members of the party arrived and one of them 'excited almost to frenzy rushed down the precipice at the imminent risk of her life.' Miss Webster, however, was in a fairly inaccessible spot and she couldn't be reached for some time.

A local surgeon arrived on the scene and with his help the injured woman was dragged out of the river and resuscitated. She was then hastily taken back to her hotel, but the shock she had experienced was apparently so great that she died within two hours. An inquest was then held and the local coroner found that death was due to 'concussion of the brain' brought on in her fall.

Watersmeet has claimed other victims since then of course, but still is one of the most attratctive walks in the whole of North Devon - if traversed with common care.

North Devon Journal 11.10.1990

38. MAN SACKED OVER PENNY

Today we hear of numerous cases where employees have sued their old employers for unfair dismissal. In the past things were very different as a case from 1848 shows where an unfortunate postman was sacked over the princely sum of one penny.

The story began in November 1847 when Rebecca Howe, a widow of Northam, wrote a letter to her naval son and gave it to her daughter Rebecca to be posted. The younger Rebecca waited until the local postman, Simon Lake, passed by their house and gave the letter to him along with a penny for a postage stamp.

Three days later she was surprised to have the letter come back from London stamped 'Returned for postage' and in order to find out why went to the head post office in Bideford. Here she saw Mrs Lee the postmaster's wife who didn't seem to think much of the case and who, rather innocently perhaps, told Lake to repay the penny to Mrs Howe – and even lent him the money to do it with! Mrs Howe wasn't satisfied with this and took her case to the magistrates who committed poor Simon for trial on a charge of 'embezzling the sum of one penny.'

The case was heard in April 1848 with Simon pleading 'Not Guilty.' Mrs Howe gave her evidence first including the rather surprising fact that Lake not only took the letter but was also the one who returned it to her – hardly the act of a guilty man one might think. She was followed by Mr Lee the postmaster who agreed that Lake had to collect letters and postage on his rounds as part of his job. When Lake gave him Mrs Howe's letter it had a stamp on it – but one that had already been used. He sent it to GPO headquarters in London for checking and they returned it demanding that a new stamp be used.

He was followed by his wife who related how she had given Mrs Howe her penny back on behalf of Lake, who said at the time 'he did not mind paying the penny' though whether this was just to settle the argument or because he was guilty wasn't stated.

Lake's defence lawyer argued rather lamely that the penny given to him was not to cover the cost of a stamp but was 'in the nature of a gratuity for his trouble in taking the letter from Northam to Bideford' – and thus he couldn't be guilty of embezzlement.

Surprisingly the jury preferred to believe this and found Lake not guilty. The judge then discharged him but added 'he hoped also he was discharged from the post office' which does seem to have happened. No nonsense then about having the stigma of crime removed merely because a person was found innocent in court! One wonders who would dare sack someone today merely over a penny?

North Devon Journal 3.9.1992

39. ALL FOR THE SAKE OF AN OPEN FIRE

Today the majority of us have central heating in our houses and open fires are a seasonal luxury. With such fires becoming less common the old occupation of chimney sweep is declining. Just over a hundred years ago in 1875, one branch of the trade was stopped by law – that of sending small boys up chimneys with a brush to clean them as they crawled to the top.

The 'trade' was one of the worst amongst the Victorian child labour groups. Boys as young as five (the smaller the better was the rule) had to climb the narrow, soot lined chimneys of our ancestors' houses, completely in the dark. Their life expectation, not surprisingly was short and a whole range of horrific diseases often came their way. It was a vile job yet North Devon has two intriguing links to it – one to its continuation and one to its abolition.

The first is via Sir Francis Molyneux Ommaney who was elected MP for Barnstaple in 1818 and 1820. Little is known of him except that he seems to have been a reactionary of the worst kind.

In 1819 a bill was introduced into Parliament to outlaw 'climbing children'. Ommaney stood up in the House and denounced the bill as 'a measure of injustice likely to do great harm to the public,' on the ground that 'the poor boys now employed...must be deprived of subsistence.'

When questioned further the MP added a weird claim that the boys were usually 'the children of rich men begotten in an improper manner.' One is left wondering if Ommaney saw chimney sweeping as some sort of punishment for being a rich man's bastard. Not withstanding the Barnstaple MP's opposition the bill was thrown out when it reached the House of Lords.

North Devon's second connection with the trade was through Charles Kingsley. Famous as the author of *Westward Ho!* and founder of Bideford's tourist trade he also wrote the classic story *The Water Babies*. Published in 1863 the book, although presented as a fantasy, did mobilise middle-class opinion against the use of 'climbing boys' through its sentimental depiction of boy sweeps escaping their job to live cleanly under water.

The Act of Parliament which finally outlawed the vile trade was passed in 1875 under the patronage of the Earl of Shaftesbury. Kingsley had unfortunately died in January of that year so did not live to see the successful outcome of this parliamentary action but one wonders what Ommaney would have thought!
North Devon Journal 1.3.1990

40. ART OF POTTERY GOES BACK A VERY LONG WAY

One of North Devon's longest established industries is pottery making. Brannam's of Barnstaple is the most famous of our present pottery firms, but in recent years many small art-potters have established themselves in the area to keep the local tradition healthy.

Amongst the most important potteries of the past (now long gone) was the 'Old Pottery' in Bideford's North Road. At one time the road was known as Pottery Lane and it seems the works closed around the turn of the century after the second of two disastrous fires within three years.

A decade or so before this the whole pottery was sold as a going concern and at its sale a detailed inventory of its contents was compiled which still survives. It was drawn up by E. Fishley of the Fremington Pottery, himself a member of the famous family of potters.

He began by listing the huge stock. There were, for example, 36 dozen size 13 earthenware pans and 37 dozen size 4 pans – these pans included both soap and 'Welsh' ones. There were 49 dozen size 26 pitchers and 15 dozen yellow pitchers, 116 dozen 4 inch and one dozen 18 inch flowerpots. As well as these everyday items there were smaller numbers of more specialised objects: rhubarb and seakale pots, edging tiles, seed, bread and salting pans. Also listed on the inventory were 'sundries' such as vases, fountains, closet pans, hyacinth pots and chimney pots.

All these wares would have been hand-made and all indicate a much greater level of domestic self-sufficiency than we have today. Domestic life then, as now, was centred around the kitchen so it is fitting that many dozen 'ovens' were listed. These were the old 'cloam' ovens found today built into chimney sides and often bearing the maker's name.

The last section of the list was taken up with the simple machinery and tools of the pottery. Thus there was £2.50 worth of flint used for adding to the clay to produce very hard ware. As to the clay itself – there was a pound's worth at the works and another £13 worth at Fremington awaiting shipment to Bideford. The 'pounding troughs' and a 'pug mill' used for preparing the clay appear in the list as do various moulds, scales and a pipe-making machine with its dies – this last being the single most valuable item at £4.

The pottery kilns are not valued – presumably they were classed as fittings – but seven kiln rakes and eight fire pikes were. In addition there was '500 furze in field and yard' valued at just £2. These were bundles of dried furze used for firing the kilns and a source of much trouble to neighbouring householders who were rightly worried about having such inflammable material near their property.

The total of the inventory came to £162.7s.11½d – a tidy sum for those days but not excessive – showing perhaps how the old Bideford pottery industry had declined since its heyday in the 17th and 18th centuries.

North Devon Journal 26.5.1988

41. THE ART POTTER WHO LIKED TO MAKE CROCKS

North Devon is famous for its pottery – a fame nurtured over the last three centuries. One of our famous potter families were the Fishleys of Fremington.

In December 1899 the *Art Journal* published an article dealing with this pottery and its wares. The Fremington pottery had been begun, it says, 'by Mr Fishley's grandfather and father who turned out large earthenware pans for use in the Devonshire dairies.'

The grandson, however, had artistic leanings and, though self-taught, invented an ornamental type of pottery he called Fremington Ware. Although this sold 'as fast as he makes it he still considers the chief business of his life to be the making of pots and pans.'

The main selling point of the 'ware' was its iridescent glaze, mainly a rich green, which 'the Fremington potter prides himself none can beat.' Apparently he was very careful not to reveal the secret by which it was produced. The *Art Journal* illustrated some of his pieces, amongst them the famous puzzle Jugs – so called because of the difficulty in drinking from them.

Fishley had adorned these with 'quaint legends' such as:

'Within this jug there is good Liquor,
Fit for parson or for vicar.
but how to drink and not to spill,
Will try the utmost of your skill.'

Fishley had also turned out some more ornate pieces decorated in graffito or scratch work. This is where a thin layer of white clay was 'slipped' over a brown clay piece and a design scratched though. After firing the design appears in brown on a white background. Fishley had won a silver medal at a pottery exhibition for some of his designs which included ornate hunting scenes.

The Fremington potter sold this pottery at Barnstaple market where, every Friday, he took 'a cartful' to sell to locals and visitors alike. Other lots went via the railway to London and 'various parts of the kingdom.'

The article ended with a sketch of the potter's home in Fremington. At that date there was a vine growing through the dairy roof and a rose covered archway through to the shed where Fishley produced his work.

His wares are now very collectable and rising in price. At least one book is being prepared which covers the North Devon 'art' potters of this period.

(This was published in 1990 by Audrey Edgeler under the title *Art potters of Barnstaple*)
North Devon Journal 2.2.1989

42. 'BUY BRITISH' EXHIBITION

Barnstaple isn't thought of as an 'industrial' town, yet in 1926 the local companies got together to stage the Barnstaple Manufacturers' Exhibition.

Held at the new demolished Castle House (near where today's telephone exchange is) some twenty companies displayed their products in order 'to educate the public to buy British goods instead of foreign' and thus help reduce unemployment.

A long report in the *Journal* details the various exhibits. Shapland and Petter and the Barnstaple Cabinet Works put on a display of furniture which included a bedroom suite in walnut made from a tree grown at Tawstock.

The Derby Lace works also had a sizable display. The report noted that 'plain net lace' was the traditional product but now new 'brown, bleached and fancy nets in a variety of designs' were being introduced. Next to the lace display was one from three local glove works where the whole process of tanning, cutting and sewing was illustrated.

Visitors could slake their thirst at Dornat and Co's display where a large variety of mineral waters were being sold. Intriguingly one part of their exhibition was 'a display of old bottles which have been employed by the firm at different stages since 1850.' Dornat's site is now occupied by the new library.

One Barnstaple firm, the Lorna Doone Rustic Works, produced seats and tables. The firm were noted as employing men disabled in the First World War. Two other companies produced 'portable buildings'. One was C. R. Dunning's of Newport who actually supplied complete bungalows.

The other two major exhibitiors were very different. One company, Messrs Blackwell and Sons of Cross Street claimed to be the oldest established basket makers in the West Country. The other firm, the Manufacturing Concrete Works Ltd, were described as a 'comparatively new industry.'

It is interesting that out of the variety of companies mentioned here most are gone, a few have changed name and products and just one or two are still going in recognisable form. One wonders when the manufacturers of Barnstaple will have another show in order to encourage us to buy British?

North Devon Journal 16.8.1990

RELIGION

43. A PROHIBITED BOOK WAS READ IN THE CHURCH

For some reason best known to itself Torrington has a long history of arguments and disputes in its churches. Recent events over the 'Black Madonna' and the British Legion are nothing new. In 1583 many of the parishioners were scandalised by finding one of their number reading a prohibited book in church.

Alexander Barry, a councillor, had gone to church one Sunday and sat next to William Edmondes, a servant to Mr Chappell. He noticed Edmondes reading 'a little booke' and asked 'I pray you, what booke have you?' Edmondes replied 'It is a catechisme' and passed it over.

Barry read a little and soon realised that 'it contayned popishe doctryne' – a serious matter at that date – just five years before the Catholic Armada sailed for England. When Edmondes asked for the book back Barry refused to return it saying he was taking it away 'because it contayned matters against the queen's proceadings.'

Poor Edmondes then whispered something to his other neighbour, a fellow servant named Humphrey Reynolds, who told Barry it belonged to Anthony Coplestone – Humphrey's master, a local gentleman. Barry still refused to give up the book and took it home with him. Here he read it and saw his initial suspicions were confirmed. He rushed back to Torrington and showed the mayor and his fellow councillors. They called in the magistrates and set the investigation in action.

The news spread rapidly and Chappell called his servant Edmondes and told him to take off his 'livery' (ie his servant's uniform) and then promptly hauled him off to see the mayor. Edmondes, however, took fright and bolted before he got there. The mayor ordered the parish constable to search for him but he could not be found.

Cheated of their real suspect, the magistrates questioned Humphrey Reynolds. He now said that the book was in fact Edmonde's own and had nothing to do with his master at all. He admitted helping Edmondes make his way to Bideford and from there to Exeter, adding that he still had his friend's clothes.

This seemed to settle the matter – presumably a message was sent to London to warn the authorities of this dangerous book-carrying Catholic.

North Devon Journal 28.7.1988

44. WHEN A WHOLE CONGREGATION WERE FINED

The 17th century was a time of great religious upheavals which culminated perhaps in the Civil War. Even after the fighting had finished religious battles continued – nowhere more so than in Bideford and Northam.

In about 1648 a group of Bideford people signed a 'covenant' to form themselves into an independent or non-conformist church in direct opposition to the Church of England. This 'covenant' was renewed in 1658 when 53 signed it including the then mayor.

With the return to the throne of Charles II in 1660 the previous religious tolerance of Cromwell began to be eroded and the non-conformists began to be hounded by the church authorities. Records are scarce but in June 1670 five Bideford constables surprised a prayer meeting at the house of Mistress Sarah Dennis, taking the names of all present and charging them with holding an illegal meeting. The minister John Bartlett and Mistress Dennis were fined £20 while the remainder of the congregation were fined 25p each.

Six months later Bideford churchwarden John Hill wrote to the Bishop of Exeter crowing over a similar attack on the 'Northam ffanaticks'. He also mentioned 'a crew of them in this town' who had been brought to order by the action of the law.

There was a raid on a prayer meeting in the house of Samuel Johns in 1671, where over 40 had their names taken. The preacher was called Thomas Handcocke, but a note on the original court record says he 'is since fledd out of the precincts (of Bideford)...and cannot be found.' Fines came to £41.50 – a very large sum at that time.

In August of that year John Hill again wrote to Exeter saying that the Bishop's orders concerning various 'disorders' in Bideford Church had been received and publicly read out by the vicar. The 'disaffected' in the town, however, denounced them as lies and ignored them.

Interestingly, a religious census in 1676 showed Bideford to have 2,500 church members and 96 non-conformists, while in Northam the totals were 1,200 and 100.

The battles between the two factions gradually died down and in 1689 the new King William passed his Act of Tolerance which legalised religious freedom. Five years later the Bideford congregation opened their first chapel which later grew into the still existing Lavington Church in Bridgeland Street.

North Devon Journal 25.1.1990

45. GIVING AID IS NOTHING NEW

Among surviving parish documents of Tawstock occurs a list of payments that is headed 'Briefs.' A brief was an order issued by the king for a charitable collection to be taken for some deserving cause. It was sent to each parish and on a particular Sunday the parish clerk would stand at the church door collecting any donations.

Much as occurs today, collections were taken for disaster victims. Thus the Tawstock list begins with a brief dated January 20 1660, 'for the Inhabitants of the towne of ffremington towards their losses by ffire the some of one pound three shillings and ffive pence.' Other payments that year were 37p to Watchet, 39p to Milton Abbas in Dorset and 54p to Ripon.

Many briefs were the result of fires – always disastrous in those days of thatched wood houses and open hearths. Most were for a named town but occasionally other details are given. Thus, in 1678 Tawstock sent 54p to Wen in Shropshire 'who had their church and steeple burnt.' That same year 37p was 'Collected for Edward Shaply of Clovelly who had his house and goods burned with fire.'

It is obvious that local appeals elicited a far more generous response than places far away. In 1692, for example, the large sum of £1.44 was collected for the 'sufferings by fire at Chagford' and £1.79 went to Northam in 1676 – though what it was for isn't recorded. Similarly, in 1669 £1.77 went for 'Marcha' in Cornwall 'upon ye Bishops entreaty' and in 1678 33p was sent to 'a hospital in Cornwall'.

Some collections went to odder causes. An undated brief from the 1670s went to 'John Sanger of the parish of Bishopps Tawton to Relieve him out of Prison.' Presumably John was jailed for debt and his neighbours were doing their Christian duty and bailing him out!

In 1681 £1.15 was collected to pay for the release of seamen 'Captive in Algiers'. The Mediterranean pirates of this period actually made a good living capturing merchant ships and ransoming their crews.

By far the greatest sums, however, were collected for fellow protestants from the Continent made refugees by Europe's civil and religious wars. In December 1686, the then massive amount of £5.63 was collected 'Towards the french breife for the french protestants'. And 18 years later £4.16 was donated 'for ye reliefe of the poor Refugees of ye Principality of Orange.' This was the last brief to be noted in the Tawstock records.

One other group of briefs deserves to be mentioned: four in 1665, all collected 'for the Sicknesse' – this being the plague then devastating London and beginning to spread into the provinces. One can imagine the horror it caused at that date even in distant North Devon and the inhabitants of Tawstock answered these requests with gifts totalling £9.72.

When one considers such briefs went to every parish in England and Wales it is obvious the system could provide very useful sums of money – and all this at at time when communications and banking facilities were primitive in the extreme. One can only marvel at our ancestors' humanity.

North Devon Journal 23.3.1989

46. BISHOP IGNORES PLEA TO STOP WEDDING

In the middle of the seventeenth century one John Pugsley was parish clerk of Barnstaple. Doubtless a pious man he also had to be a person of utmost respectability – a position sadly weakened by the actions of a relative if we are to believe a letter written by John in November 1669.

The letter is only eleven lines long and was addressed to the office of the Bishop of Exeter. Not only was it short, it was to the point. 'In case any person should come to you for a licence for the old Edward Slee of Barnstaple these are to give you notice that he is a person incapable of marriage by reason of age and infirmityes.'

The licence referred to was, of course, a marriage one and Pugsley's interest seems to stem from the fact that his daughter-in-law Mary Shoppleth had married an Edward Slee some twelve years previously and had borne him three children. I say 'an Edward Slee' as there were two, father and son, living in Barnstaple at that time. From the phrases used by Pugsley I think we are dealing with the elder Slee.

Pugsley's blunt letter continued, 'I much doubt that he is not himself, neither knowes well what he doth for he is betrothed unto several persons and will be as ready to do the same with others.'

The clerk's ire seems to have been raised because Edward was 'a very ill liver, usually drunk every night and light Queanes will marry him only for his estate to the ruine of poore little ones if not prevented.' Presumably the wonderful expression 'light Queanes' refers to women of easy virtue whilst the 'little ones' were the children of Edward junior who were all under 12 at the time.

Their mother had died the previous month and clearly Edward junior had brought pressure on his influential relative to try and thwart his father's remarriage. After all, if his apparently senile father married again then any expected inheritance might easily be wasted by a 'light Queane' of a stepmother!

Pugsley finished his letter by saying 'This I thought to give you notice of assuring you that I will make good all the premises' i.e. he could prove what he said.

Unfortunately for the parish clerk his erstwhile relative seems to have ignored any advice he might have given him (as did the Bishop) for we find in the Barnstaple parish register for 12 January 1670, the record of a marriage between Edward Slee the elder and Mary Towten. Edward the son must also have remarried for another seven children were credited to him over the next 17 years.

North Devon Journal 4.1.1990

47. REPORTING BACK TO THE BISHOP

Every organisation spawns its own bureaucracy – the church is not exempt. In the past, with poorer communications, it was difficult for the Bishop to keep track on the state of the churches in his diocese. Every few years, however, the Bishop sent the local rural deans on a 'tour of inspection' of the churches within their deaneries and many of these reports have survived.

The Barnstaple deanery has an interesting collection beginning in 1674. In Barnstaple at this date the dean found 'that ye walle which keep up the rising earth in the Churchyard, is in many places broken downe, so that ye graves with the dead Bodies are in danger of falling into the allyes and thoroughfare.' Overcrowding in St Peter's graveyard was a perennial problem until the 1840s when it was finally closed.

The next surviving report dates from 1734-5 – a year marked by strong storms. At Chittlehampton the windows in the North aisle were 'much damnified by the Late Storm.' The glazier had 'Repair'd some parts of Them and The Other were order'd by the Wardens to be repaired as soon as the Freestone was brought from Bristol.' Similar damage was also found at Yarnscombe.

Bells feature in the 1751 report from Yarnscombe where the dean noted 'An Old Gentlewoman that loved Ringing left by her Will Six Pounds a year towards ye keeping this Tower & Bells in good Order payable out of an Estate in a neighbouring Parish. The Churchwardens receive that sum of money annually, but shamefully neglect her beloved Tower.'

Another common problem was the non-resident vicar. In the eighteenth-century many clergy had two or more livings (parishes) and usually lived in the richest one leaving their poorer parishes to manage how they could. At Huntshaw, for example, it was reported in 1751 that the parsonage was 'not for to be inhabitated' – even though the vicar had two livings and a rich estate in South Devon.

A different state of affairs existed at Filleigh where Lord Fortescue was building a new rectory in 1751, which 'will be a very handsome one' noted the dean. The Lord had also built a new church and when the dean pointed out that it contained neither a board showing the Commandments or the royal coat-of-arms as it should have done Fortescue replied that 'he thought it would be no ornament to his new church to have any.' Doubtless the dean and his Bishop let Fortescue off!

North Devon Journal 9.2.1989

48. WHEN YOU COULD FACE PENANCE IN FRONT OF A PARISH

I have written before about the old consistory or church courts which had the power to try offenders against the moral code. Punishments varied from public penance in front of the whole parish to excommunication. If one could avoid a consistory court appearance one did.

The chance survival of a letter written in November 1675, shows how one man escaped the clutches of the morality court. Philip Blinch, churchwarden of Alwington, wrote to the Bishop of Exeter from his home in Buckland Brewer.

He had been 'earnestly desired by a neighbour of maine (mine)' to intercede on behalf of 'A honest Seaman' called William Liell who came from Alwington. William had been told 'he shall be in great

Trouble in your Court for that his wife had child 13 weekes after hee was married.' This was clear evidence of the 'crime' of sex before marriage and carried the penalties outlined above.

William had met his wife 'About a Ladyday 1674' but at that time he was 'Shippt for Newfoundland' (i.e. signed on for a voyage) and, the winds changing, he had to join his ship before they could be married. On the vessel's return the couple came to 'A Chapple in Buckland Brewer called Bulkworthy' and were there married. The clergyman who officiated gave William a 'cirtificate' as evidence of the marriage. The child followed 13 weeks later. Its baptism can be found in the Alwington parish register where on January 1 1675 Elizabeth the daughter of William Lill (sic) was baptised.

This was the only baptismal entry that year, which shows how small the village was – and probably how widespread was the knowledge of the embarrasingly short period between marriage and motherhood!

After reciting all this, Blinch got to the point of his letter when he wrote 'If there by Any Process of Summons gone out of your Court for this Will leill of Alwington that you will recall them and discharge him for this business.' Blinch even went so far as to offer to pay any expenses the court may have incurred in the case, which was very magnanimous.

I have searched the records of the consistory court but can find no mention of this case, so presumably Blinch's pleas were listened to and acted upon. This letter has, however, survived to give us a brief glimpse of human nature in the late seventeenth century.

North Devon Journal 7.12.1989

49. PEALING BELLS ECHO HISTORY'S SOUND

Amid all the hurly-burly and noise of everyday life we seldom notice any extra sounds yet there is one that does stand out – the ringing of church bells. If we could go back a hundred years of course the music of the bells would be one of the few loud noises that we heard – no cars, drills or radios then. In those days the bells were rung for a variety of reasons – not just weddings and on Sundays as now seems to be the case. To see the range of occasions we can turn to the churchwardens' account books of South Molton covering the late seventeenth-century.

Thus in 1684 82p was paid 'for Ringing when the King was

proclaimed.' This refers to the naming of James II as the new king on the death of Charles II. In 1690 25p was paid 'for Ringing by order when the news came that their Majesties fleet had beaten the French.' This celebrationary peal for military victory was a common occurence and was a rapid way of spreading news. The 'Majesties' referred to were the protestant William and Mary who had replaced Catholic James in 1689.

Only a week after this naval victory the bells were set ringing again, at a cost of 40p 'when the news came of his Majesties happy Victory in Ireland.'

This was the battle of the Boyne, the last battle at which an English king was actually present and one celebrated in Northern Ireland to this day. A special peal of bells was ordered in September 13th, 'when the newes came of his Majesties arrivall from Ireland.'

If these were one-off occasions an annual 'ringing' occurred on November 5th to celebrate the capture of Guy Fawkes and the escape of Parliament from his intended explosion. Another annual celebration was Coronation Day when the bells rang for a long period.

And so the entries continue. In 1691 three special peals are recorded 'at the news of the surrender of Lemerick'; 'on the news of his Majesties Return from Flanders' and 'by the Mayors order it being a Thanksgiving day.'

To round off the century and this article I can quote one final entry. A 'general meeting' of the parishioners of South Molton was held in 1700 to set new rates of charges for the ringing of the bells to celebrate baptisms, weddings and funerals. It was agreed that 'every person who shall cause the Great bell of Southmolton aforesaid to be rung or tolled shall pay to the Churchwardens or Sexton for the time being for the use of the said Towne and parish the sum of one shilling.' (5p)

The prices have gone up since then but when next you hear church bells pealing just take a few seconds to consider how many times they have rung out and on what occasions – from village weddings to national celebrations. If history can be said to have a sound then surely it is the sound of bells.

North Devon Journal 29.6.1989

50. RUDE WORDS FROM A VICAR

Readers of Trollope's novels will know well the intrigues and feuds of Georgian clergymen (and their wives). The theme is a common one in the literature of that period and is based on the many eccentric or high-handed churchmen of that time. Here in North Devon we had similar characters as the following story from Ilfracombe will illustrate.

The vicar of the town in 1802 was one Emanuel May who appears to have been a very pugnacious gentleman. One Sunday in October of that year he was taking the afternoon service with the help of his churchwarden Nathaniel Vye. At one point 'just before the general confession' he suddenly said to Nathaniel 'Sit down wilt'.

Evidently surprised by this curt order the churchwarden asked if the vicar was addressing him. In answer the Reverend May gave him a 'a threatening look and raised his fist up and exclaimed to the said Nathaniel Vye, 'Sit down wilt' adding 'Do'st mean to interrupt me in my duty. Thee deservest to be put into court'. Poor Nathaniel couldn't think of any adequate answer and so kept quiet.

A little time later, as the congregation began leaving, the vicar asked the parish clerk Cutcliffe Greenslade if he had heard the churchwarden making a noise during the service. Greenslade said no, whereupon the vicar 'in a very brawling and angry manner and with a loud voice at the same time stamping with (his) foot on the ground' replied, 'I'll make thee forswear thyself or I'll trample thee under my feet.'

The clerk and churchwarden weren't going to put up with this sort of treatment and took their vicar to the bishop's Consistory Court accusing him of 'chiding and brawling and behaving in a very irreverent manner.' This court was a church body which had control of clerical misdemeanours and it is from its records that the details of this case have come down to us.

It was, however, notorious for its slowness and this case was no exception. Judgement wasn't passed until January 1804, when the Bishop of Exeter announced in a very elaborate, signed and sealed document that the Reverend May was absolved from all blame in the matter. He further added that the costs of the case were to be shared between the vicar and the churchwarden (now confusingly called Nathaniel Vye Lee).

A small ripple in the life of the church as a whole, but one wonders what tidal waves it set up in the small community that was Ilfracombe at this date!

North Devon Journal 16.2.1989

51. A MEMORY OF RELIGIOUS SECTS LONG PAST

The history of religion in Britain is nothing if not dynamic. Groups come and go – Catholicism gave way to Anglicanism which in turn soon divided into various sects such as the Baptists and Methodists. These sects then subdivided further – some to the point of virtual (and actual) extinction. One such group was the Primitive Methodists who could trace their beginnings back to around 1810 in the North of England.

They were, however, a keen missionary church and soon spread to the South West. Their first flowering in North Devon came sometime in the late 1820s. This early congregation was well scattered – in 1830 for example 60 members were listed at Barnstaple, 14 at Bideford, 6 at Mortehoe, 3 at Pilton and 5 at Eastleigh. By 1851, however, when a census of religious groups was taken this small sect had melted away.

One of the few reminders of their presence that we still have today is a small register of baptisms preserved in the North Devon Record Office. This has recently been transcribed by Michael Wickes, a local genealogist and this reveals some intriguing details.

Of the 37 entries the first ocurs in March 1834 and the last in September 1848. In each case the child's name plus those of his parents is given. In addition the father's occupation is also listed and these have a wide range – from mason to potter and from hairdresser to ship carpenter.

In 1837 Samuel Burt a 'lace-twister' of Pilton baptised his son Richard. Samuel would have worked at the local lace factory then in operation. A John Darke of Bideford 'miner' appears in 1848 – presumably he worked in the culm mines (later the paint mines) at East-the-Water. Most of these men were working class but at least one 'gentleman' appears as well as an early 'engineer' in 1844.

Such registers were all required to be sent to the Registrar General at London in 1837 when Somerset House was established but, for some reason now lost, this one never went and such a local survival is very rare. This means that the sixteen baptisms prior to

1837 are unique records – no other copy of them exists outside North Devon.

Just to round off the story the Primitive Methodists did try to re-establish themselves in the South Molton area in 1858. A new baptismal register was begun and this ran until 1888 when the sect appears once again to have disappeared. This second register has joined its forerunner in the North Devon Record Office today.

North Devon Journal 19.1.1989

52. NO FUN AT CHRISTMAS FOR OLD JUNIUS

Scrooge may have replied'Bah, humbug!' when asked his views about Christmas, but most people look forward to the celebrations and enjoy them when they arrive. At least one North Devonian, however, seems to have shared Scrooge's rather morose views on Christmas and all that went with it. His name is lost to us as he comes down to posterity only by his pen-name of 'Junius' although we do know that he lived in Appledore.

On December 3 1829 the *Journal* printed a letter from 'Junius' on the front page. It begun by pointing out that the choirs from several parish churches usually met in December to practice the hymns they would be performing in church on Christmas Day itself.

'Junius', however, could not help but 'wondering in this enlightened age, how a rational and discerning public can countenance such a burlesque on true religion as this dreadful practice holds up.' The dreadful thing he refers to wasn't the singing of hymns but 'the direful effects, almost in every instance attendant on this practice.'

This associated action was carol singing for money and the way the singers took a seasonal drink at every house at which they called. The writer reckoned this rendered 'the greatest number of them intoxicated e're the morning dawns, as to be incapable not only of attending service but of coming out of doors on the Christmas Day.'

This wasn't all that annoyed 'Junius'. Apparently, the choir meetings where the carols were rehearsed were also scenes of 'feasting, drinking and dancing and a train of vicious amusements always attendant on such meetings.' Are choir practices still so interesting today one wonders?

The high jinks at the meetings were paid for in two ways – partly from the money collected by the carol singers and partly from a sub from the parish officials i.e. from the rates – which was another cause of irritation to 'Junius'. Clearly our ancestors took their carol singers much more seriously than we do today.

'Junius' finished his letter with a wonderful outpouring 'Let not the nabobs of our parishes talk of morality, the degraded state of the lower order, the need of magisterial authority and so on, till they put their hands to crush instead of encourage a system so baneful in its effects as a village wake.' So now you know what was the main threat to the peace and stability of Georgian England – carol singing and its obviously associated evils.

North Devon Journal 21.12.1989

53. GREAT SCOTT ADDED 'STYLE' TO CHURCH

The nineteenth century was the great period of church renovation and alteration and such refurbishment was tackled with that energy common to all Victorian undertakings. One such church that experienced this transformation was Fremington in 1867. Prior to this date the church was described as looking 'dilapidated and unsightly' on the outside and 'deformed and defaced in a manner truly barbarous' on the inside.

The vicar, the Rev. J. Pigot, not being able to afford complete rebuilding decided to renovate the church. He may not have been able to afford rebuilding but he did secure the most famous church architect of his age, Gilbert Scott, to oversee the work.

Scott favoured a 'simple' style and this is what he used at Fremington. The old pillars were replaced with 'elegant pointed arches' and 'two equal aisles' were reinstated to their original form of a nave and a single aisle. A new roof was added. The tracery in the windows was renewed and new stained glass inserted. The old floor tiles were removed and replaced with 'Godwin's coloured tiles' whilst a new wrought-iron rood screen was erected. At the same time the tower was repointed and repaired.

As well as altering the structural details new church furnishings were added. A newly embroidered altar cloth prepared by a Mrs Beard of London was given to the church by Mrs Clarke, and an oak lectern and communion rails were also presented by well–wishers.

During these changes a fifteenth-century stone pulpit was found buried and after some necessary work was reinstated under Scott's direction. Also found were some ancient wall frescoes but these crumbled soon after exposure. All these alterations cost about £1,650 and were carried out by the Barnstaple firm of Dendle and Pulsford.

The opening ceremony was on Tuesday June 11 1867 and £30 had been collected 'for the purpose of giving a cordial and hearty reception to all who should come.' In the event 'no less than a thousand persons were entertained by the Committee of Management in a barn adjoining Fremington House.' In addition to feeding the adults a special 'Children's Entertainment' was laid on when 'the whole of the children in the parish were bountifully supplied with tea and cake.' This was followed by 'a number of rural sports.'

A real holy-day or holiday for the villagers, and doubtless one that was affectionately remembered for many years by the churchgoers of the parish.

North Devon Journal 9.6.1988

MILITARY

54. ROYAL PRINCE WHO LIVED IN BARNSTAPLE

The English Civil War had been raging for three years in 1645. King Charles was fighting a losing campaign and his enemies were beginning to close in on him. For safety's sake he decided to send the Prince of Wales (later Charles II) to Royalist Barnstaple.

The town had begun the war as a Puritan stronghold but had changed hands several times and still contained many who had no sympathy for the King and his son. In addition, the local Royalist garrison were becoming notorious for their bad behaviour, leading to disaffection among many supporters. This was the town to which the 15-year old Prince rode in June 1645.

He entered via Bear Street where he was met by the Governor of the town Sir Allen Apsley who escorted him to lodgings in the High Street house of Grace Beaple, widow of Richard, a prominent merchant (his monument in St Peter's church is one of the more grandiose). She was 64 and though her husband had reputedly been a Puritan she apparently volunteered her house – a decision that was to cost her dearly.

The Royal party stayed a month. Little is known of how the Royal heir spent his time, though, as a historian writing 70 years ago quaintly put it, the Prince left a 'lasting pledge of his affection' to the town in the form of a baby daughter who 'has herself left descendents, some of whom occupy' distinguished positions.

When Cromwell's armies destroyed the Royalist cause the Barnstaple Puritans turned on Grace Beaple and pillaged her house of goods worth, it was claimed, £2000.

Grace lived until 1650 and on her death was buried in Barnstaple churchyard. Her granddaughter Elizabeth Eastmand had to wait another 10 years until Charles II took his throne to get any redress – and then she received only £200.

As far as I know this is the only occasion a member of the Royal family lived in North Devon. If it ever happens again let us hope it isn't due to a Civil War!

North Devon Journal 6.4.1989

55. SENTENCED TO SERVE TIME IN THE NAVY

Much has been written on smuggling, yet hard facts are not that common. In 1832 a notable case was reported in the *Journal* when the smugglers were captured.

It began in January when a vessel appeared off Ilfracombe and, being hailed by customs officers, her captain said she was laden with china clay on her way to Gloucester. The officers, however, were suspicious and decided to watch her.

Their suspicions bore fruit when that night they saw a small boat come ashore and land 64 kegs of brandy. The smugglers were met by a party of local farmers but before any business could be transacted three customs men rushed up and seized the spirits. Unfortunately another boat load of smugglers arrived, attacked the officers and 'severely beat them.'

The customs men, however, grimly held on to their booty, until the smugglers rowed back to their ship and made off to Appledore. Here, at Graysand, they landed the remainder of their cargo before disappearing. It was not to be their night as the Appledore customs men had been warned and were waiting. Another 22 kegs of brandy were seized. Later that same night the officers searched a house in Heanton and captured a further 16 kegs.

Within a week the vessel returned to Appledore but this time it was itself captured by the customs officers and brought in triumph alongside Bideford Quay. Here she was revealed as the *Gazelle*, a fast yacht belonging to a 'local gentleman'. Doubtless the officers thought they had broken this particular smuggling ring, but within a few weeks they had seized another 300 kegs of brandy near Appledore!

At the beginning of April 1832 the first group of smugglers were tried and sailors Archibald Winter, John Parry and James Hervey were sentenced to serve five years on board 'one of His Majesty's ships of war' – which gives an insight into conditions in the navy at that time. Accomplice William Oatway, an Appledore rope-maker, was fined £100 – a massive sum in those days.

The group were followed two weeks later by three more 'of the persons concerned in the late smuggling transaction at Graysand near Appledore' being fined £100 each. If they couldn't raise the money, they were to serve time in Exeter jail. A week after this, a father and son named Williams from Appledore were also fined £100 each.

So ended this particular group of cases with three men forcibly impressed into the Navy and six others fined £600 between them. The risks for smuggling were clearly high – but undoubtedly so were the rewards.

North Devon Journal 26.4.1990

56. SUFFERING ON THE CRIMEAN BATTLEFIELDS

The Crimean War of 1854-56 was fought a long way from Britain on the southern shores of Russia. It was notable for the stupidity of the Generals, the sufferings of the troops and the huge death toll from disease rather than wounds. It was the first was in which the men taking part wrote home in any numbers – and had their letters printed in the papers. Many make fascinating reading.

The first letters home were the death and wounded notices – of Edward Major, son of the Town Crier in Bideford, shot in the arm and left for dead for 30 hours before being rescued; of the son of the Rev. Karslake of Meshaw, killed in the first battle of the war; of Archibald Clevland of Tapeley House, Instow. He was killed in the disastrous Charge of the Light Brigade and Tapeley House still has on show the bloodstained uniform he wore on that day.

The first 'real' letter printed appeared in the *North Devon Journal* on Decembr 21 1854 and was from William Mountjoy of the Rifle Brigade. He wrote to his parents in Barnstaple from a hospital in Scutari saying, 'I have been very bad this winter, but I hope I shall soon get better. The men are dying fast with diarrhoea, and I am nearly crippled with the rheumatism, with lying on the wet ground.' These comments are typical of many of the letters.

A letter from Richard Radford of the Naval Brigade arrived in Bideford, 'We had hard work the first fortnight, dragging up guns and mounting them in the batteries and at night we man most of them. I am happy to say we have only lost five men from our ship's company.'

T. Fairchild wrote to his father at Newport, Barnstaple, complaining 'We have no covering as yet but a bit of canvas. There are wooden houses sent out; but what use are they when the roads are impassable, and we can't get them up?' Another unsigned letter in that issue speaks of 'visiting the poor fellows in the cholera hospital, who were lying, cold and comfortless.'

Bearing this in mind it it hardly surprising that sailor William

Friendship, could tell his parents in Torrington in the same month 'We have lost 30, only two have been killed by the enemy, the rest died from exposure on the shore.' William Dingle of the 47th Regiment of Foot, also from Torrington, wrote to his father 'It is enough to break one's heart to see the wounded.'

It was about this time that Florence Nightingale set about improving the wretchedly primitive hospitals that served the Crimean forces. She had been prompted in part by such letters as I have quoted. A letter from Lieut. J. Grier, of the 88th Regiment of Foot to his father at Georgeham in May 1885 shows the impact of this woman and her nurses, 'I heartily wish this horrid war over. Miss Nightingale and the Sisters of Mercy are angels...'

North Devon Journal 23.4.1987

57. THE DRUMS OF WAR CALLED FAR AND WIDE

One of the things about history, as compared to the present, is that you know what the eventual outcome of any event is going to be. Reading local newspaper reports of the outbreak of the First World War one is struck by the excitement and near-jollity of it all. War with Germany was declared on the evening of August 4 1914 and by the next day North Devon was alive with preparation.

At Bideford the Territorial soldiers were called up and 'Every man turned up promptly.' We read how 'a great cheering crowd accompanied them across the Long Bridge to the railway station,' where they were seen off by the Mayor 'amid a fusillade of cheering.' At a meeting of the town's Church Lad's Brigade, 17 of the older members volunteered as 'special constables' and 43 offered to join the Local Civil Volunteer Corps. Ilfracombe saw its Army reservists called up along with the 125 men of the Ilfracombe and Lynton Territorial battery who left for a 'secret destination'.

Barnstaple, as the HQ of the 6th Battalion of the Devon Territorials, saw a large influx of men coming back to the barracks. In addition the local yeomen who made up the troops of the North Devon Hussars came trotting in. Many of these men lived on outlying farms and only learnt about the outbreak of war from Boy Scouts who had been sent to fetch them. The first troops to actually leave Barnstaple were 40 Royal Navy reservists from Appledore.

At South Molton the 12 members of the local territorial company assembled in the Square, shook hands with the Mayor and marched away with a local band at their head.

Amidst all this activity other things were also happening. Some 14 German and Austrian men were arrested in Ilfracombe, Lynton and Westward Ho! where they had been working as waiters or musicians. This was probably as much for their own safety as for military security – though a rumour did sweep South Molton that the local reservoir had been poisoned by German agents! The deputy mayor of Barnstaple appealed to people not to hoard food on the optimistic basis that the war would soon be over.

If only they had known! It was to be four long years before the carnage was over. The first North Devon casualty appears to have been Captain Thomas Wickham, a Bideford Territorial man who was serving with the Manchester Regiment. His death reported in the first week of September 1914, where it was also noted that he left a widow and child, was to be the first of many in North Devon.

North Devon Journal 12.5.1988

58. WE'RE INVADED BUT DON'T WORRY

North Devon newspaper readers must have been somewhat alarmed to see the headline 'Capture of Northam' in their papers in March 1916. Reading on they would have been relieved to find that the village had been captured by a mock 'German' force as part of an exercise involving the local Volunteer Training Corps (the First World War version of the later Home Guard.)

It began with a 'motor scout' racing into Bideford and reporting that the 'Germans' had landed at Westward Ho! under cover of fog and had over-run Northam using the Square for their supply dump. These invaders consisted of the Bideford Cadet Corps (the Church Lad's Brigade) and local Boy Scouts from both Northam and Bideford.The VTC bugler did his stuff and the Bideford men were soon gathered 'fully armed' in the Market Square. They quickly marched to the 'level crossing under Raleigh' (part of the old Appledore-Westward Ho! railway) to join the Northam contingent.

Here the officers decided to split their men into small groups and attack Northam Square from various directions and 'try their best to destroy the ammunition and stores with petrol bombs.' After having the plan outlined to them the men set off, and their officers followed later, but right from the start the plan degenerated into virtual farce.

The 'very reliable scout' leading the officers got lost and eventually had to break his way through a fence to regain the road.

Unfortunately he lost 'the greater part of his nether garments' whilst another officer 'fell head first into a ploughed field'. The group then had to take shelter in a ditch and 'were frightened out of their lives by two heifers...jumping up under their very noses.' To cap it all they made 'another detour and nearly fell into a pond at the bottom of a field.'

Whilst the officers were thus engaged the men were also in trouble. Most of them had been captured and those who hadn't were hiding in Northam churchyard unable to time their attack as they couldn't see their non-luminous watches!

In the end four did get through and 'destroyed' the dump – though if this had been real life no doubt they and most of Northam would have been destroyed. Those captured were all mud-caked with many tears in their uniforms – evidence of their difficult cross-country scramble.

The 'Germans' didn't do much better as they not only let four 'attackers' get through but most of them were extremely cold as their overcoats had been 'left in billets through oversight'. To strengthen their defences they erected barbed-wire entanglements across the main road to 'hold up everything passing.' This they did very successfully and 'although some members of the fairer sex became 'annoyed' they were allowed to proceed with expressions such as 'maze fules' etc.'

The evening's exercise finished with a few words from Sgt. Major Collins who 'congratulated all on their keeness and on the work executed that evening.' He added, rather sarcastically 'They would now all grasp the difficulties entailed in carrying out night operations.' No doubt they did – and one can only be thankful that the real Germans didn't invade Westward Ho! at night –though if they had been as amateurish as the cadets perhaps it wouldn't have been too bad.

North Devon Journal-Herald 13.2.1986

The building is unrecognisable today but this is the original Saunton Sands Hotel taken sometime before 1934

A lovely painting of the *Sewell Jane* a 3 mastered schooner built in 1868 at the Rolle Canal Company's shipyard at Sea Lock two miles above Bideford Bridge

Taken around 1939-40 in the Bethel at East-the-Water, Bideford this shows a few of the evacuees who were sent to North Devon following the outbreak of war.

One of the most photographed sights in North Devon – Clovelly with its donkeys.

The May 1956 launch of the tug *Sceptre* at the P. K. Harris yard in Appledore

The inaugural trip of the Bideford, Westward Ho! and Appledore railway, – with brass band in attendance. The large building in the background is still there – unlike the much loved railway.

The North Devon Hussars in Boer War period uniform on the move through **Northam Square**

THE NORTH GATE HOTEL

Barnstaple - North Devon

Tel : Barnstaple 2856

Members British Hotels
& Restaurants   Association

Blockbusters now occupies the site shown on this 1950s advertising postcard. The back of the card stated that bed and breakfast was £1.25, which seems very reasonable.

Bideford Cattle Market just off Honestone Street in 1926 with the mayor and various dignitaries present, note the black sunshade.

A sad, derelict 3 masted square rigger off Appledore prior to its being broken up – possibly in the 1870s. Alongside is a local ketch and barge. The ship is possibly the *Delaware*.

BARNSTAPLE.

THESE are ſtrictly to prohibit and forbid all Perſons whatſoever, from henceforth, from placing or lodging any Hogſheads, Barrels, or other Casks, of Wine, Oyl, Brandy, or Tobacco; or Bags of Wooll, or any other Goods, Wares, or Merchandiſes whatſoever, in the *Walk*, or *Exchange* on the Quay of *Barnstaple* aforeſaid, or againſt the Pillars thereof; and alſo all Boys, Girls, and other Idle Perſons whatſoever, from playing in the ſaid *Walk*, or climbing about the Pillars thereof. And the Conſtables and Beadles, and other Officers of this Town are hereby order'd to be careful in preventing the ſame accordingly. And it is further ordered by this Corporation, That whoſoever ſhall diſcover any perſon or perſons whatſoever that ſhall hereafter ſcore, mark, *or grabe* any Letters, Figures, or Names on the Wainſcot, Seats, or Pillars of the ſaid *Walk*, or any way deface the ſame, ſhall receive as a Reward for ſuch his or her *Information* the Sum of *Five Shillings*, to be paid by Mr. MAYOR for the Time being, and the Offender and Offenders herein ſhall be *proſecuted* both by *Action of Treſpaſs* and *Indictment* with the utmoſt *Severity* of *Law*. And it is *further ordered*, That this *Order* be *forthwith Printed* and *Publiſhed* about the *Town*, and *after affixed* in *ſame public Place* on the *Walk*, and againſt the *Guild-hall* of this *Town*. And it is *further ordered*, That *twice a Year for ever hereafter* (to wit) on *Lady-day* and *Michaelmas-day*, except when on a *Sunday*, and then on the *day following*, at *the Hour* of *Eleven* in *the Forenoon, the Cryer do* republiſh *this our Order* round the *Town* in the *uſual manner*, and *afterwards affix* the *ſame* in the Places *aforeſaid*.

Dated this Seventh Day of October, Anno. Dom. 1714. And in the Firſt Year of the Reign of his Majesty King GEORGE.

An old postcard which proves that vandalism is nothing new!

Barnstaple Fair about 1930 when it was still held on the Strand. The helter skelter is approximately where the Civic Centre stands today

Barnstaple in calmer days. The old North Devon Athenaeum in the Square with a cab driver's shelter in the foreground

Barnstaple High Street. The top storeys of the shops are still recognisable today even if the street level frontages have been replaced with aluminium and plate glass. Note the Summer boaters.

It is hard to visualise the Exeter Road in Braunton as ever being so quiet – today the area is full of shops and traffic.

Ilfracombe – a wonderfully framed and atmospheric view taken in its Edwardian heyday.

The Quay, Appledore long before the recent extensions – no problem with global warming then

Instow. The entire staff of the railway station including the white bearded stationmaster came out for this shot. The platforms still exist on one side of the Tarka Trail.

An early photograph of Wrafton showing a good example of a cob and thatch building

Bucks Mills in the more leisurely 1950s before the roads became so busy as today.

The pebble ridge at Westward Ho! looking taller and wider than it does today.
The photograph was taken around 1880.

A fascinating view taken when the original 'iron bridge' at Weare Giffard was being widened –
an operation only just recently repeated.

Taken outside the present-day Plough in Torrington this shows the first group of recruits at the start of World War I. How many returned home?

In *North Devon History* I wrote about Joseph Becalick who lived in a chimney – and here is a postcard of his home – though who would want to send this I can't imagine.

North Devon Hussars in camp 'somewhere in North Devon'. Note the white gloves in the top pocket of the man standing on the left.

A wonderful photograph taken in the 1930s of the construction of the road bridge by today's 'Puffing Billy' at the base of the hill up to Torrington – the old medieval Rothern Bridge is in the background.

59. NORTH DEVON CELEBRATES THE OFFICIAL PEACE

Recently I wrote about North Devon and the effects of the outbreak of the First World War in August 1914. Nearly five years later in July 1919 the official 'Peace Day' was held. The two days in fact, were much the same, being marked by public events and excitement – although by 1919 this was heavily tinged with grief over wasted lives and maimed bodies.

In Barnstaple, the day began with a huge civic procession walking along the flag-bedecked High Street to an open-air concert in Rock Park. The event ended with the planting of a commemorative copper beech tree near the bandstand. This was followed by a sports meeting attended by nearly 8,000 people, who were serenaded by a band of newly demobilised servicemen.

In the afternoon a tea was given to some 2,500 local children in the Pannier Market – 'an event that will long live in the memories of the participants' wrote one reporter. The food was supplied by Bromley's Cafe and each child was presented with a souvenir medal to mark the day. The town's Mayor gave a speech celebrating the peace and 'the greatest victory probably ever won by this country and over one of the most treacherous foes we had ever fought.' The day ended with a fireworks display at Trafalgar Lawn.

In Bideford a massive religious sevice was held in Victoria Park followed by the provision of a dinner for 800-900 demobilised men in the Market Hall – paid for out of the rates. A sports event and a fancy dress parade were also held. At Ilfracombe a salvo of 21 rockets were fired from Lantern Hill followed by a 'drumhead' service. Hundreds of children, each bearing a flag, marched up Capstone Hill and arranged themselves to form the word 'Peace'. Tea and sports concluded their day.

Every village in North Devon was permeated with the mood for celebration – although Torrington somewhat oddly held a steeplechase as well as the more usual carnival. In Lynton the council chairman paid special thanks to the village's 'Crutch Makers Group', whilst children at Stoke Rivers each got a souvenir in silver. Chittlehampton held dog and bicycle races and at Bratton Fleming the local Christy Minstrels paraded the village at 5.30 am 'with bugle, mouth organs and various other instruments.'

Each village finished the day by lighting a bonfire on a prominent hill and it was reported that at one time an observer on Codden Hill could see 21 such fires. So ended the public celebration of peace – a fitting end to 'the war to end all wars.'

How many of the celebrants could have thought that within 20 years another such war would break out?
North Devon Journal 14.7.1988

60. TOWN FEELS THE EFFECTS OF WAR

North Devonians were spared the worst effects of the Second World War, but that isn't to say that the war had no impact on life in this part of England. Because of censorship, records are scarce but the minutes of the Bideford Borough Council reveal fascinating aspects of the 'People's War'

Over the six months November 1942 to April 1943 the council discussed a whole range of war items ranging from the collection of iron railings to help the war effort in January 1943 to the damages inflicted on the Quay wall by an unnamed 'Naval Vessel' in November 1942.

Much time was spent on the fire guards and deciding on the location of static water tanks for use in bomb attacks. In conjunction with this much energy went into providing air raid shelters and policing the 'blackout'. This was generally well run but in December the borough librarian complained that during blackout 'disturbances had been caused by children in the reading room.'

Money was tight but the single largest expenditure was on setting up a 'British Restaurant' in the Pannier Market to supplement others in Gunstone and Allhalland Street. This was a council-run cafe providing hot food at cheap prices to children and war workers. People I have talked to who recall its fare weren't too enthusiastic about it. The actual restaurant was opened by the mayor in December 1942.

The drive to provide adequate food was complemented by propaganda to grow more. The 'Dig for Victory' campaign was reported on in the same month with a note that all allotment holders were to be strongly encouraged to produce more.

At the same time the council were trying to cut down waste wherever possible. In November the council split the proceeds of local rag and bone salvage between the dustmen and its own coffers. Two months later the town clerk noted that 'the ministry' had decreed it 'was an offence to waste fuel.' An earlier fuel economy campaign had been run by the Women's Voluntary Service and they were congratulated on its success.

In among all these serious items the Council found time to welcome to one of its meetings US Private Murphy from the town of Biddeford in Maine, USA – an early example of twinning?

Rather more oddly they considered a complaint by one Frank Bright who alleged that local Workers' Educational Association adult education evening classes were spreading 'anti-Soviet propaganda.' The local organiser denied the accusation and the council took no further action.

The most intriguing reference is a very short note to the effect that Mrs D. Hewson was to be paid £1 'in connection with the preparation of the 'War Book' as recommended by the invasion committee.' Presumably this was a guide to what should happen were Bideford to be invaded. Does any reader know any more about this volume or what it contained?

North Devon Journal 20.9.1990

TRANSPORT

61. A PERILOUS COASTLINE

North Devon's rugged coastline has claimed many victims over the centuries. One such disaster occurred in November 1840 when the *Collina* of Bideford came to grief on Baggy Point.

The 180 ton ship was the property of the famous local shipowner Thoman Chanter and was captained by Henry Potter of Braunton with a crew of five. It had sailed from Bideford in the summer to take a shipload of emigrants to North America and then loaded up with timber to bring home.

Setting out from Quebec in the middle of October it had a good voyage across the Atlantic and all was well until it neared the bar of sand across the entrance to the mouth of the Taw and Torridge. As it arrived the wind was blowing a 'strong West North West and a heavy sea running.' The local pilots didn't bother to help the captain as they knew him to be skilled navigator who was well acquainted with the local tides and currents. For some reason, however, the captain didn't attempt to cross the bar immediately and this was his undoing.

The wind rose quickly and the ship was carried past the estuary mouth. In attempting to gain the comparative safety of Croyde Bay the *Collina* struck Baggy Point and 'almost instantly became a total wreck.'

The master and four of the crew tried to launch a small rowing boat but the now mountainous seas washed them all overboard. One of these men was luckily thrown back on to the ship and he survived, along with a cabin boy, by desperately grasping on to the rigging which still stood above the level of the waves. They were rescued by people lowering ropes down to them.

The following morning revealed a scene of devastation – the whole of Croyde Bay was covered with smashed and broken timber. The first on the scene were the 'wreckers' or looters but they were scared off by the arrival of armed Customs officers.

The bodies of the captain and three of his crew were washed up and an inquest, rather obviously, returned the verdicts of 'accidental death.'

An auction of the timber was due to be held on the beach but another storm following hard on the heels of the first washed most of it out to sea again and it was lost.

No one knows how many ships Baggy has claimed but today, when vessels no longer have to hug the coastline because they lack radar, the toll has fallen dramatically. Let us hope it remains a rare wonder.

North Devon Journal 6.2.1992

62. NEW RAILWAY LINK NO ONE WOULD HAVE

Before Bideford lost its rail link some years ago, new travellers to the town were often surprised to find the station on the eastern side of the River Torridge. It made a walk or taxi ride across the town's Long Bridge a necessity.

In 1898, however, a scheme was put forward to remedy this. It came from the developers of the Bideford, Westward Ho! and Appledore railway who were then busily laying track along Bideford Quay.

A packed town meeting was held to discuss the issue in the town hall under the chairmanship of mayor W. Braund. The directors wished to extend their railway to the Long Bridge in order to 'take another new bridge across to the south western station' at East-the-Water, said railway company spokesman, a Captain Molesworth.

This new bridge would parallel the old one and the Captain 'should have thought that the council would have jumped at the proposal.' He added that a line along the quay would not obstruct either the promenade of the bridge traffic and the proposed new bridge would be designed to allow boats easy access up stream.

A councillor, Mr Pollard, put the council's point of view that such a scheme was 'antagonistic to Bideford, both in its commercial value and artistic aspect,' a statement greeted with applause from the audience. He went on to claim the development would 'drive residential people from the neighbourhood' and 'spoil the river for boating.' A Mr Tedrake stated bluntly that 'the scheme would really only benefit the promoters.'

Among all this opposition few voices spoke out in favour. Mr Lowman, solicitor to the rail company was one. The rail lines would be level with the road and 'when a train was coming, a bell would be sounded to warn pedestrians', he pointed out, but this didn't appease the objectors.

The last words came from a Mr Tattersill who thought nothing should be allowed to detract from the beauty of the old bridge, 'the town's main attraction.' He was joined by Alderman Narraway, the oldest councillor, who reminded the meeting that the 'town council had been unanimous in their decision to oppose the scheme.' He closed the discussion with the simple statement 'the Long bridge was the soul of Bideford'.

The resulting vote was an overwhelming defeat for the rail company's plans...which seemed to consign the idea into limbo forever, as I can find no further reference to it in succeeding years. It is interesting to speculate what might have happened if the new bridge had been built.

North Devon Journal 10.8.1989

63. A BY-PASS THROUGH THE VILLAGE CENTRE

There has been much talk over the proposed Braunton by-pass, mainly over the perceived damage it will do to the nearby Great Field. In 1923, however, a new road was opened which actually went right into the heart of the village. It is still in use today and runs from the central crossroads to the Ilfracombe - Barnstaple road. It took a year to build and cost just £8,700. The navvies were all out-of-work ex-Servicemen employed under a special Devon County Council scheme.

Although it appears so central to the village today, it was actually a 'by-pass' in that it took all the traffic that had previously 'passed through the narrow and winding Church Street.' It also, apparently, cut five minutes off the Barnstaple-Ilfracombe journey.

The opening ceremony was on October 15 1923, when Lord Portsmouth attended in his capacity as chairman of the county council roads committee. He cut the ceremonial rope across the road – an event marked by several speeches, all reported in the local press at great length.

Alderman Yeo began these speeches by remarking that 'there were not many present who did not know something of the terror of going through Church Street, with the rush of cars.' He went on to strike a very contemporary note when he mentioned traffic jams of up to 45 minutes in the height of summer. This occurred when 'no less that 47 cars got in the street at the same time.' Demolition of houses to widen the street had been suggested but rejected on the grounds of a local housing shortage.

Lord Portsmouth stressed the vital importance of new roads in

Devon to cater for the growth of motor traffic. Roads weren't just of local interest, he said, but 'were becoming matters of imperial importance' – whatever that meant! Not only that, but Braunton, 'an ancient and interesting parish' as he termed it, would benefit from the extra 'beanos, charabancs, picnic parties, empty bottles and more wastepaper bags.' Clearly nothing is new.

A vote of thanks to Lord Portsmouth was proposed by Captain Incledon-Webber who took the opportunity to press the county council 'not to allow large signs and advertisements along the road.' He was seconded by a Mr Dunn who said, rather obviously, that 'although Braunton was not the centre of the universe, it was a very important centre indeed.' Speeches over, the party went to have tea at the local 'council school'

The report of the ceremony ends with a note that Messrs Evans had opened a garage at the junction of the new road and the Square. Now replaced by a modern shopping precinct, it rings a topical note with all the present discussion on the provision of garage facilities on the North Devon Link Road.

North Devon Journal 30.11.1989

64. CATALOGUE OF ACCIDENTS TO SHIPPING

All of us create records – diaries, letters, bills – but few of us make a conscious effort to preserve them. One class of people do however – solicitors, as a professional duty, look after many documents. Mr P. Sims of the old-established Bideford firm of Bazeley, Barnes and Bazeley showed me one of the older documents in his care.

Created by Henry M. Bazeley over the years 1903-31 it is a large volume of sworn statements concerning accidents to shipping at or on their way to North Devon ports. Ship captains apparently had a legal duty to make such statements – probably for insurance purposes.

The first entry is typical of most. On January 26 1903, Thomas Symons master of the 472 ton barque *Serena* of Plymouth came to the solicitor's office to record that he and his 11 man crew had left London on January 2 with a cargo of bagged manure for Appledore. In Bideford Bay 19 days later they 'experienced very stormy weather' and were forced to 'slip' the anchor – cut it loose, and run before the wind to Appledore Pool. They just made it and anchored there but then 'she parted her chain and collided with the schooner *Annie Davis* doing damage to both ships.'

In April of the same year James Fowler master of the Bideford ketch *Sylph* appeared to tell his story. His boat had been carrying coal from Lydney and approaching Bideford the 'rudder head became fouled' and the boat stranded on the South Tail bank near Appledore. A flare was sent up and the lifeboat responded. Unfortunately the lifeboatmen refused to help the *Sylph* even though Fowler offered them £30. A local gig boat then arrived and with its assistance the *Sylph* limped into harbour.

Other accidents recorded in this volume are the occasion in 1906 when the *Mary Barrell* schooner was damaged through being overloaded with clay at the Cross Park Quay in Bideford. Unfortunatley for her master she settled 'on a rock' and was thus severely strained.

In 1918 the large steamship *Natura* ran into an unknown steamer off Hartland during thick fog. The *Natura* was sounding her whistle at the time, 'but the whole thing happened so suddenly it was impossible to avoid collision.' The other ship didn't stop and the disabled steamer just made it to the Taw Estuary to be beached on Instow sands.

Some 108 maritime accidents were recorded in this book by Mr Bazeley. Each account is signed by the ship's captain and many are fascinating stories of courage and determination though casual understatement appears common to all the masters. One wonders what other archival treasures are waiting to be found in the solicitors' offices of North Devon?

North Devon Journal 18.2.1988

LAW AND ORDER

65. WHEN THIEVES WERE BANISHED FROM TOWN

You have almost certainly never heard of an eyre, yet in 1238 one was held in Devon. Briefly, it was a sporadic visit made by royal judges to hear civil and criminal cases traditionally tried by the king or his representatives. The idea was to settle such cases and give a show of royal strength to the provinces.

The 1238 visitation has been transcribed and printed, giving fascinating glimpses of our ancestors of 750 years ago. Each area or 'hundred' of Devon sent 12 men to Exeter to present evidence in each case. The cases brought varied greatly, as did the punishments, which ranged from fines to banishment or death.

The most serious crime was murder, as where Richard, the clerk or vicar of South Molton was presented for killing one Roger Necke. He was arrested by his own congregation, but escaped and fled to the town's church for sanctuary. While there he agreed to be banished and so was let go. The trial came to the eyre only because the victim's wife Agnes was charged with being an accessory. She was found not guilty, however, and released. Clearly the story behind this case was more involved than we can know today.

In Barnstaple, Ralph Cluter had pulled Emma Gulke from a window and in falling she was so badly injured that she died seven weeks later. Ralph fled, was outlawed and had his goods seized by the court.

Accidental deaths were also dealt with by this court on the basis that the king could levy a fine on the community for any fatality. This was a lucrative source of income and many examples are listed. Martin le Bedel drowned with his horse in the Torridge; Geoffrey, son of Ranulf, fell over Torrington bridge and was mortally injured and in Barnstaple 'Richard the roofer' fell on his own axe and died.

Other cases were for rape with another South Molton clergyman, 'Arnold the deacon', being presented for raping Margaret, daughter of William de la Wheie. At the trial it was revealed, however that Margaret was in fact the deacon's mistress and that the attack followed a 'lovers' tiff.' The case still went ahead and was proved and Arnold was hauled off for punishment by his bishop.

Theft cases were common, the offence being a hanging one if the goods were valued at more than five pence. In most instances the thief was discovered, fled to the nearest church for sanctuary and chose banishment rather than execution. Thus Robert the Irishman stole a tunic, was detected and fled to Ilfracombe Church while the oddly named Henry Biwlf ended up in Fremington Church.

In addition to these cases there were some oddities, as with one at Berrynarbour where seven men discovered a chest full of treasure and disappeared with it rather than surrender it to the authorities, much to the latter's annoyance.

The oddest case concerned Matilda Clapper, of Shebbear, who, with her daughter Gillota, was seized by Walter Lupus, put in chains and taken to Kentisbury where they spent the entire autumn helping with the harvest before being released without payment of any kind. In court Walter claimed they were his feudal villeins or slaves, who had run away. In fact, Walter was found to have overstepped the mark and was fined £1.

Colourful times. One can say only that we live in slightly more law abiding communities today – and I for one am happier for it.
North Devon Journal 5.10.1989

66. OATHS TO KEEP LAW AND ORDER

Today our lives appear to be dominated by bureaucracy. We may look back to the past and envy their assumed freedom – yet our ancestors were just as hemmed in by officials with their rules and regulations.

Amongst the archives of Barnstaple Corporation exists a book dating from around 1550 listing all the oaths to be taken by newly appointed town officials. Some 34 are listed and many of these posts were for more than one person so one gets some idea of the minuteness of control exercised in the town some 400 years ago.

Fittingly, the first oath listed was for the Mayor who, amongst other duties, swore to repress all heresies and treasons, prevent riots and routs, silence common scoldsters and slanderers and act fairly to both rich and poor. In this he was helped by the aldermen or senior councillors, the coroner and 24 ordinary councillors.

These duties were funded from money looked after by the Town Chamberlain or treasurer and collected by a group of bailiffs and rent collectors. Much of this money came from the market tolls and there was a Clerk of the Market who not only levied charges but also ensured that food was sold at reasonable prices and that it was 'wholesome for man's body'.

Slightly odder posts were those of Fewrer of Weights and Viewers of Market Days. The first of these inspected the various weights used by retailers and if found wrong, destroyed them. The Viewers were to see that no non-freeman, i.e. non-locals, could sell goods in the market.

Another major group of officers was concerned with local industry. The first of these was the Yarn Weigher who checked on weights of woollen yarn sold, an important post at a time when wool was of such great value to the West Country. A more specialised position was that of the Searchers and Sealers of Leather who checked all boots, shoes and clothing made of skins to ensure that no poor quality goods were sold. Similar officers were the Viewers and Weighers of Karseys and Cloth who dealt with finished textiles. They had to check that no illegal materials were included and that the dyes used were fast.

One very important group was that of the 12 constables who were the 'police' of the town. They were aided by the Beadle of Beggars who saw that 'noe sturdy beggars or vagabonds be wendrying, loytring or begging openly in the streets or at men's doores.' An Overseer of Strangers kept a check on the more well-off newcomers to the town.

Few of these officers survive, but the Mayor still takes an oath on taking office, much as the office holder has done for the last 600 years or so – a marvellous example of English historical continuity.
North Devon Journal 26.7.1990

67. BIGAMY BY MISTAKE?

One in three of all British marriages end in divorce today - a figure that worries many. They point to the pre-war years when divorce was relatively rare. If we go back even further into the nineteenth century we find that divorce was virtually unknown, if only because every legal break-up of a marriage needed a private Act of Parliament!

For most the only form of 'divorce' was separation which was then followed by a bigamous remarriage. Bigamy was rarely detected but one case that was occurred in North Devon in the 1840s.

The trial was held in March 1841 at the Devon Assizes in Exeter and the evidence was simple. On April 17 1828 Thomas Prust had married Mary Pillman at Hartland Church. The couple lived happily enough at Hempsgate, Hartland, for three years and then moved to Bideford.

In 1832 Mary's brother John Pillman came to Bideford and returned to Hartland with his sister, leaving Thomas behind. A few weeks later Mary sailed for North America without telling her husband and that was the last they saw of each other for the next eight years. After that time she returned to England and went to stay with her father at Hartland where she discovered that Thomas had remarried.

His new 'wife' was one Eliza Stone of Torrington and his bigamy was proved in court when the parish clerk of Torrington produced the parish register recording the 'marriage'. On the face of it the case was straightforward. Thomas was obviously guilty and deserved punishment but he fought back.

He called as a witness Robert Rayley a carpenter who was on the same migrant vessel to North America as Mary and distinctly recalled her sharing a cabin with the ship's master Captain Harper. Robert couldn't swear that adultery had happened but the imputation was obvious. In addition, Thomas pointed out that the law allowed remarriage if a husband or wife had not heard from each other in seven years (very necessary at the time when travel was hazardous and communications poor.)

His lawyer added that bigamy charges were usually brought by the second 'wife' but it had not happened in this case. Indeed, Eliza 'had no resentment; she did not feel he had done her any wrong.' The only reason the lawyer could see for Mary bringing the case to court was to extort maintenance from her husband, even though she had deserted him and not attempted contact for years.

There was little Mary's lawyer could say to soften these points. He tried to allege that it was Mary's brutal treatment at the hands of her husband that had caused her to leave, but the judge refused to accept uncorroborated evidence.

The jury only took ten minutes to find Thomas not guilty and he departed the court a free and legally married man. Mary apparently disappeared to Scotland - presumably herself free to remarry. A strange legal decision, but perhaps the best one for all concerned.
North Devon Journal 27.12.1991

68. TRANSPORTED FOR LEAD THEFT

Thieves today, it seems, concentrate on money, jewellery or electrical goods – all high value, easily portable goods. In 1827 however, a case came before Barnstaple Quarter Sessions in which three men – Thomas Ward, James and John Greeny – were charged with stealing 10lbs of lead piping from house fronts in the town. James and Thomas, who were youths, pleaded guilty, but John, James's father, said he was not guilty.

They had been caught when James Harvey, an accomplice, turned informer and gave evidence against them. They had all met by the lime kilns along Taw Vale and 'prowled about till between 11 and 12 o'clock'. They then split up with Harvey being stationed in front of the churchyard gate and the younger Greeny at the corner of Joy Street.

When these two gave the all-clear, Thomas and John went to Mr Moon's 'and twisted off the lead in question from the pipes which convey the water from the roof of his house.' They repeated their plundering next night when their victim was Robert Rice of Cross Street. The stolen lead was hidden in both cases in the churchyard.

Unfortunately for them an apprentice, Emmanuel Cottey, noticed the lead as he went through the churchyard and carried it home to show his master.

After hearing the evidence in the Moon case the jury didn't bother retiring and 'immediately returned a verdict of guilty' for all three. In the second case all three men pleaded guilty and were found so by the jury.

The judge then 'strongly reprobated the conduct of the elder Greeny' who he saw as 'the contriver of those robberies and the seducer of his own son and those two other youths into the paths of vice and immorality.' As ringleader he received the heaviest sentence – seven years transportation to Australia after being publicly whipped through the streets of Barnstaple. His son and Thomas Ward were sentenced to six months hard labour in the town jail. As to the informer, the judge warned him that if he ever appeared before the court again he would certainly be transported.

The punishments may seem severe to us – after all, who would steal drainpipes today? In the past, however, public justice was extremely severe and offenders could expect little mercy...whatever they stole and how little its value.

North Devon Journal 30.3.1989

69. PICKPOCKET TRANSPORTED TO AUSTRALIA

Many people today complain that prison sentences and punishments in general aren't harsh enough to deter would-be criminals. One can ask, however, what was it like in the past when the law was far more oppressive?

A case from October 1830 illustrates the question well. In that month the Barnstaple Quarter Sessions took place in the Guildhall where the only trial was that of Charlotte Noy on a charge of stealing a watch from Mr F Drake. He was a yeoman or small farmer from Braunton who had come to Barnstaple Fair in the previous month to enjoy himself. This took the form of getting drunk and he was in this condition when he met Charlotte in The Fuller's Inn in town.

The meeting took place some time after midnight (licencing laws were very flexible 150 years ago!) when Charlotte asked Drake to treat her to a glass of gin. The befuddled yeoman agreed and as he went to the bar she accompanied him and 'put her right arm round the prosecutor's waist and with her left hand, drew his watch from his pocket.' Unfortunately for her, a man called George Symons saw the theft and appeared in court to swear that he had.

Charlotte was asked if Symons was telling the truth, she said no, adding 'that he was a false swearing blackguard and would swear his mother from her grave!'

Another witness, James Gibbs, then appeared to relate how he had found a watch in the North Walk (where the Civic Centre now stands) the next morning which Drake identified as the one stolen from him.

The judge summed up the evidence and the jury quickly found Charlotte guilty. The judge then told her that 'till a late period the crime of which she had been found guilty was deemed a capital offence' i.e. one could be hung for it. Now, however, the judge could set the penalty but as he reckoned that picking pockets 'was a crime of such frequent recurrence', he sentenced her to the 'severe punishment' of being 'transported beyond the seas for the term of seven years.'

Charlotte was then taken to Exeter Jail on her way, in chains, to the hulks in Portsmouth or London where she would have waited for a ship to take her to Australia to serve her sentence. The punishment seems excessively harsh to us today – seven years exile in what was a wild country for stealing a watch – but it was better than being hanged!

Clearly, such savage sentences hadn't deterred poor Charlotte, though, as many writers have remarked, many poverty stricken Britons actually welcomed transportation as an improvement to their life and we know that many convicts did well in Australia. One wonders what happened to Charlotte. Did she marry a colonial and have children, and are her descendents still living in Australia today, all owing their existence to a watch stolen in a Barnstaple pub 150 years ago?

North Devon Journal 23.11.1989

70. PRISONERS TAKE THE LAW INTO OWN HANDS

It is often strange how the present mirrors the past. The recent riots at Strangeways and other prisons were not different, except perhaps in their intensity, from earlier disturbances in our jails. In North Devon today of course, we have no prison. In 1834, however, Barnstaple did have one and also had some prisoners' disturbances.

The prison was in the Square where the new road now joins the roundabout. Constructed in 1828 it had 14 cells and a small yard, surrounded by a 20 foot high wall.

In November 1834 the various prisoners complained about the lack of provisions they received. Bad food in nineteenth century jails was a long running complaint, but it was noted that the gaoler, Mr Blackwell, 'was proverbial for the kindness which he exercised towards the unhappy inmates under his care, and the indulgences which he afforded them,' and in all his twenty years of service had never experienced complaints about the food.

The prisoners, described in the contemporary *Journal* reports as 'these hardened and infatuated men' began by 'loudly vociferating their complaints' demanding extra food. Blackwell went to the mayor and he immediately went to the prison and 'after reasoning with the inmates', he ordered that they receive the same amount of food as the paupers in the workhouse.

This, however, didn't satisfy them and they began shouting out at the top of their voices, 'starvation', 'murder' and 'proceeded to demolish the utensils with which their prison was furnished.'

The mayor, aldermen and several other influential gentlemen went to the prison and 'expostulated with them on the impropriety of their conduct.' This, rather surprisingly perhaps, produced a cessation of their violence, but it was noted that 'they continued to manifest a sullen demeanour.'

That this disturbance was a real threat is clear when one considers that at this date Barnstaple had no professional police force. Serious rioting and violence could only be overcome by the use of the military which often led to widespread injury. It is interesting to note that only a few days later the town set up its own police force, the forerunners of today's Devon and Cornwall force. The old prison itself was demolished in 1874 having been condemned as unfit for use. A new prison was built in Castle Street, but it became redundant only four years later when all prisoners were ordered to be sent to Exeter, thus precluding any more prison disturbances in North Devon.

North Devon Journal 28.1.1990

71. WHEN IT WAS SELF HELP TO BEAT THIEVES

Several times I have written about the early police forces of North Devon – the voluntary constables, the first professional police and the 'specials' The ancient parish constables were probably adequate until overwhelmed in the late 18th century by the huge growth in crime associated with a massive growth in population.

The professional police, on the other hand, didn't enter the scene until the 1830s in North Devon. So what filled the gap between the decline of the constables and the rise of the police as we know them today?

In the towns the local merchants and traders banded together to form mutual help groups to combat the criminal. At this time prosecutions were expensive and often not followed up for want of money – the 'protection societies' as they called themselves existed to provide the money – as well as offering rewards for the capture of law breakers.

Records of such groups are rare but I have come across three local ones – the Bideford Association for the Protection of Property, the Ilfracombe Protection Association and the Barnstaple Association to Prevent Horse Thefts.

I have noted three references to the first of these. In January 1825, the pottery works of Thomas Anthony had been broken into and four 'square iron bars' stolen. A reward was offered by the Bideford Association. The thief wasn't caught though the iron was traced to a blacksmith at Abbotsham who had brought them in good faith.

In 1836 Bideford got its first paid policeman, Elias Palmer, and, although very capable the association members evidently decided to keep their group going. Palmer made a few important arrests and in August 1839, we read, 'At the late annual meeting of the Bideford Association for the Protection of Property, it was ordered that a silver medal should be awarded to Elias Palmer police officer of Bideford, for his efficient services in the apprehending of a prisoner convicted of a felony on the property of a member of the Association, and for his general vigilance and good conduct.'

The meeting to award this medal took place in the New Inn where chairman Thomas Vellacott, a local draper, carried out the presentation. Palmer 'expressed his gratitude for the honour done him, and trusted that his future conduct would equally merit the approval and support of the Association.' One would like to know where this medal went or even what it looked like but the records are silent.

Three years later Palmer again made a notable capture – Joseph Beer of Buckland Brewer – an infamous local sheep stealer. At his trial Beer was sentenced to transportation for 14 years in Australia. The Association members again decided to honour the policeman and at their 1842 AGM had a collection to buy a silver snuff box for Palmer. Enough money evidently came in as the snuff box was purchased and engraved ready for presentation in October of that year. A special dinner was held at which Palmer was guest of honour. Palmer again thanked the Association for its kindness and one is again left wondering where the snuff box has gone today.

By this date, however, the association was losing its usefulness. Most areas had a professional police force and the original reason for the group's existence had thus gone. The association struggled on; the last reference I have found of them fighting crime directly comes from September 1861, when they offered a guinea reward for stolen property.

The association lasted at least until 1917 but by this date, and probably for many years previously, it appears to have been acting as a sort of insurance society. When it finally faded away I do not know – but it is an interesting example of a local response to local crime.
North Devon Journal 14.5.1987

72. THE FIRST BANK ROBBERY

On June 30 1839, Barumites awoke to the news that their main bank had been burgled. The Old Barnstaple Bank as it was known was situated in the High Street but the criminals had broken in at the rear via a hole in the roof. Letting themselves down by a rope they broke through another skylight to get into the main banking room. Here they tried to force open a strong box but failed and so left with just £5 in notes and some £10 worth of gold and silver.

The case remained a mystery until some nine months later when one Elizabeth Gubb was jailed in Barnstaple on a minor and unrelated charge. Just before her arrest Elizabeth had rowed with her old landlord John Day and in talking to another inmate about it let slip that John had been involved in the unsolved bank robbery.

The information was quickly passed on to the authorities who hastened to John's house and carried out an extensive search. During this they found a damaged chisel which left marks similar to those found on the strong box in the bank. On this basis John was charged with theft and came to trial that April.

Elizabeth was the main prosecution witness and told how, while lodging at John's house, she had heard him and four other men talking about 'a nice crib' (i.e. an easy target) The men then left and reappeared sometime later and shared out a pile of money.

Evidence about the chisel came from William Stribling, a local cabinet-maker, who swore that it had to be the tool used to try and break open the bank's strong box. Superintendent Steele, of the borough police, then told how he had found the chisel at Day's house.

Day's lawyer began his defence by pointing out that Elizabeth was a notorious prostitute who had kept quiet about the crime until it suited her desire for revenge. He then produced two witnesses. Mary Ann Hammett who slept in the same room as Elizabeth at Day's house, who swore that their landlord had never left the building on the day of the robbery.

She was followed by another of Day's lodgers, Louisa Besley, who swore that the chisel produced in court was not the one she saw the police find in their search. Unfortunately for Day the prosecution pointed out that both women were also well known prostitutes.

The jury took an hour to find Day guilty and he was sentenced to 15 years transportation to Australia. During the trial Elizabeth had identified another of the thieves as William Bird and he was duly tried some three months after Day and although the evidence against him was very circumstantial and he had a good alibi, he was also found guilty and sentenced to seven years transportation.

Thus ended North Devon's first bank robbery. Luckily, of course, there haven't been many others and with today's vastly increased security such crimes are unlikely.

North Devon Journal 26.9.1991

73. HAT THIEF EXILED FOR TEN YEARS

People today often moan about the perceived leniency of the law towards criminals Yet, in the past, when punishments were truly vicious people still committed crimes – a paradox that can only be resolved by saying that human nature rarely changes. A good example of this past severity comes from October 1840 when one William Nicholls was transported to Australia for ten years for the theft of a hat!

The case stemmed from an incident on Barnstaple Bridge one night in September of 1840. John Gabriel and his father William, both farmers of Fremington, had visited Barnstaple Fair then held on what is now the Civic Centre area.

Staying late they began walking home at midnight and as they crossed the bridge a man passed them and the elder Gabriel wished him 'Good Night.' Immediately he had said this the man came over to John, grabbed the hat from his head and raced away with it.

John hared off after this sneak thief. Catching him up in Maiden Lane the thief threw the hat away but was collared by another person as he ran on. John handed him over to Superintendent Steele of the borough police saying that he didn't know the prisoner and did 'not know that ever I saw him before.'

This account formed the basis of John's evidence at the trial, the only additional fact being that he had kept the thief called Nicholls in view at all times except when he bent down to retrieve his hat after Nicholls had thrown it down.

Superintendent Steele then gave his evidence, adding that while taking him to the police station he had 'wept bitterly and said someone had taken his hat as he went over the bridge.'

Nicholl's lawyer, Mr Kingdom, tried to put up a defence case saying that the identity of the prisoner could not be proved as Gabriel had lost sight of him when he bent to pick up the hat. He rather ruined this line defence by adding that Nicholls 'did not take the hat feloniously, but that the act was merely a practical joke.' True it was a 'gross impertinence' but it wasn't really a crime.

The judge then summed up as fairly as he could but the jury 'instantly' found Nicholls guilty. At this point Superintendent Steele and the clerk to the court produced evidence of a previous court appearance by Nicholls for passing counterfeit coin. Although he had been acquitted 'circumstances came out on trial which were exceedingly discreditable to him.'

The judge passed sentence saying that 'as he despaired of his amendment by any term of imprisonment in this country' he would do his duty and 'banish him to a foreign land' for ten years.

North Devon Journal 31.10.1991

74. ATTEMPTED MURDER

Violence against the police is often said to be a new symptom of our ailing society but is this true? In March 1841 a court case was heard at the Devon County Assizes when one Henry Vicary was tried for the attempted murder of Superintendent David Steele head of Barnstaple's Borough Police Force.

The first witness in the case was the Superintendent who said that on January 27 he along with police constables Snell and Chanter had gone along to the Angel Inn in Barnstaple with a warrant for the arrest of Henry and his accomplice in crime Mary Patterson, a well-known local prostitute.

They found Mary along with William and Susan Vicary in the kitchen of the pub and attempted to arrest the former. She, however, became very violent and screamed out 'Harry, come and shoot him.' Henry then appeared holding a pistol in his right hand and called out 'Stand clear and I'll shoot him.'

No sooner had he said this than he fired and Steele was thrown back against the bar. William Vicary then cried out (rather phlegmatically) 'Harry you have shot me, but never mind old fellow.' Henry replied, 'Never mind William, I hope you are not much hurt, I have another left for them yet.' He retreated up the stairs followed by the recovered Steele.

Cornering his attacker on the landing Henry pointed the pistol at him and said 'he would blow my brains out' as Steele put it. Mary

Patterson was also there encouraging Henry to shoot. Susan broke the impasse by crying that William needed a doctor. The Superintendent and his two officers took the chance to carry the wounded William off to jail where a doctor treated him for a light leg wound.

The police then returned to arrest Henry but found the house barricaded and their man gone. Steele advertised for him in the *Hue and Cry* (a police newspaper) and had 'wanted' posters printed and distributed – which led to the wanted man's capture along with Mary Patterson.

Corroborative evidence came from P.C. Snell who added that he had seen plaster fly off the wall after Vicary fired his pistol – though a later search had failed to retrieve any bullet. Dr. Tarr then gave evidence as to William's injury and alleged that it wasn't a bullet wound at all – merely a bad graze.

The defence lawyer made two points. Firstly, Henry was only responding to his friend's cries for help – he didn't realise that the men manhandling his girlfriend and sister were the police. Secondly, that the pistol wasn't loaded with a bullet but only with gunpowder and this was fired merely to scare off the 'attackers'

William then claimed that his wound came from being viciously kicked by Superintendent Steele – and not from any bullet. The plaster that was missing from the wall had dropped off 12 months before. Three character witnesses were then called but two of them didn't appear.

The prosecution highlighted William's perjury about his 'shooting' and the fact that to even fire a blank charge at another human was a serious offence. The judge agreed with this in his summing up and the jury followed his lead by finding Henry guilty of 'malicious shooting.'

The judge then sentenced him to a year's jail with hard labour. The Superintendent went on to serve for several years more in which he saw more action – but that will have to wait for another time
North Devon Journal 21.5.1992

75. FORCEFUL SENSE OF SECURITY

Devon's police force, as we see it today, dates from 1857 when the first chief constable and 299 other ranks were established by the county magistrates. This new force operated mainly in the rural areas, the old boroughs generally having established their own police some 25 years before.

The first chief was a Mr Hamilton and one of his duties was to prepare an annual report on the state of his men and their activities. His report in April 1859 was generally very optimistic and he could write, 'The force under my command continues generally to conduct itself in a steady and efficient manner' – a statement borne out by messages of support and gratitude from various parishes and individuals.

Unfortunately, not all was good news. One member of the County Police Committee asked leave to read out a petition from the ratepayers of the parish of Challacombe in North Devon. The petitioners didn't mince their words but got straight to the point stating 'That since the establishment of the County Police, criminal offences in their small parish, have increased rather than diminished.'

The allegation was backed by examples. In July 1858 two sheep were stolen from the local vicar while two local farmers, W. Huxtable of Wallover and Mr Burden had also lost two sheep apiece. Other victims lost sheep and poultry including Mr Leworthy of Challacombe Town and Mr Crang of Whitfield. This list ended, 'In no one case have the perpetrators been detected.'

The petitioners did not blame the resident policeman but reckoned 'the existing system must be faulty' in that the main work of the policeman appeared to consist of 'patrolling the roads' – work that was 'far more of a military duty and that highway robbery in the district was wholly unknown.' J.Carwithen, the writer of the petition and rector of Challacombe, ended by demanding either that the 'present force' be made more effective, or else the ratepayers should be relieved from the 'enormous increase of their county rate required for the support of a force so ineffectual as that at present constituted.'

At this date the local policeman was a '1st class sergeant' earning just £1.15 a week plus an annual allowance of £3.70 to cover the cost of his boots, oil (for lighting) and, oddly enough, any stationery he used. His uniform consisted of black trousers, black frock tailed coat and a top hat and he had to wear this for most of the year as he only got 22 days holiday including bank holidays.

Bearing in mind the difficulty of catching rustlers, the size of his beat and the lack of communication it isn't surprising that he hadn't caught the Challacombe thieves.

In fact it seems that the petitioners were more worried about the rates thay had to pay than the actual level of crime. It is worth noting that the 'enormous' rates referred to were in fact just 0.25p in the pound!

The petition was considered but rejected and the local policeman stayed in his post for some time to come, establishing by his presence a new sense of security in most law abiding citizens – even if his first year or two wasn't very auspicious.

North Devon Journal 30.7.1992

76. THREATENED BY FENIANS OF THE PAST

The scourge of the IRA seems to be always with us – yet many people think of it as a modern problem. In truth, the IRA can trace its history back to the 19th century when 'fenians', as they were then known, were planting bombs and killing people just like today.

In 1868 the 'Fenian Outrages' across Britain led to a state of near panic. In January of that year for example there was an attempt to blow up Worcester Guildhall and 14 Fenians were arrested at Merthyr Tydfil.

South Wales was closely linked to North Devon by a fleet of cargo vessels bringing coal and limestone to our area and a strongly reinforced police and coastguards were given 'strict orders to watch the coast at Ilfracombe and Appledore ' and 'more especially at Clovelly and Hartland.' This wasn't just to look out for Fenians from Wales as apparently the authorities also feared 'a landing of American Fenians.' Local fears were heightened by the reported theft of a large amount of gunpowder from the magazine of the 6th Devon Volunteers in Barnstaple but this was later denied.

This scare, however, led to the swearing in of between 300 and 400 special constables to guard the town. At a public meeting in the Guildhall it was decided to arrange the men into 'three divisions for Barnstaple, Pilton and Newport' the whole body being based around the 'rallying point' of the Guildhall.

The 'superintendent' of this force was Captain McKenzie 'the respected adjutant of the North Devon Battalion of Volunteers,' aided by three other Volunteer officers.

Within the week ten points of 'Instructions for Special Constables' were issued. These dealt with the division of the town into subsections adding that 'Sgt Major Garland will give his services to instruct special constables in the few movements recommended in the circular from the Home Office.' Weapons were limited to a truncheon each and these were to be kept at the Guildhall until needed.

Luckily for Barnstaple nothing came of this Fenian threat although two Irish suspects were arrested at Plymouth. Indeed the whole thing seems to have been a 'nine days wonder' ending in a rather limp series of letters to the *Journal* concerning the difficulties of getting insurance to cover injuries suffered in the line of duty by 'Specials' Certainly, however, the massive force so rapidly embodied highlights the patriotism of our Victorian forefathers.

North Devon Journal 17.10.1991

77. KILLER OR NOT? YOU DECIDE

Public opinion is a power for good or evil as a case from Bideford in 1887 shows.

Henry Ellis described as a 'lodging house keeper' appeared in the local Bankruptcy Court and admitted that he owed £294.4s yet had only £33 to his name. He added, somewhat weakly, that 'his was a ready money business, and he had not kept any account of the money paid or received.' This was somewhat surprising as he was also secretary of the 'Forester's Friendly Society' in the town and regularly handled large sums belonging to the members.

It was, however, the same Society that brought in the bailiffs to obtain payment of a debt of £6 owed by Ellis to them. They took away some furniture but were prevented from taking more because most of it belonged to Mrs Ellis and could not legally be taken. Indeed Mrs Ellis was a large property owner in her own right. She owned their business and had raised £800 by mortgaging other houses.

Where this money went wasn't recorded but only a month later an advert appeared saying 'Dwelling house, with the dining rooms, shop, and premises known as the North Devon Refreshment House and Forester's Hall...at the corner of Buttgarden Street and Honestone Street...now in occupation of Mrs Elizabeth Ellis.' The building still stands now occupied by the Praxis cafe.

Matters took a decidedly nasty turn. A week after the sale Mrs Ellis was dead under suspicious circumstances. An inquest was called and various people gave evidence – amongst them a servant Eliza Chapple who said, 'The deceased took her meals all right, and seemed better than usual: but I thought her a failing woman for many months.'

Henry, the husband said, 'My wife's health had been failing of late. I consider she was getting weaker inwardly, and she was often in very low spirits.' Henry's concern didn't appear genuine when it was revealed that he had found his wife lying, apparently drunk, on the bedroom floor on the night of her death – and had done nothing. All this happened on the day of his second appearance at the Bankruptcy Court – which he hadn't told his wife about.

Dr. John Duncan didn't help by admitting that 'the deceased might have died from alcoholic (poisoning), but he preferred not to give any opinion, as there were no appearances to lead to this or any other conclusion.' The jurors replied 'that it had been freely rumoured in the town that Mrs Ellis had been poisoned,' but the doctor refused to be drawn.

The jury concluded that no post-mortem was necessary and gave their verdict 'found dead' which meant nothing at all. Henry had, of course, inherited his wife's property. The contemporary papers noted that 'it is seriously proposed in some quarters to apply to the Home Secretary in order that he may exercise his authority and sanction the exhumation of the body,' buried straight after the inquest.

At Henry's bankruptcy proceedings he had claimed that 'one of the causes of his failure was his wife's drinking habits and her extravagance. He was sorry to attribute it all to his wife, but it was true nevertheless.'

Bideford Watch or Police Committee met and demanded to know what the police were going to do about the perjury of Mr Ellis – a strange charge which oddly came to nothing.

Three weeks later Henry appeared again at the Bankruptcy Court and said 'His wife had left a will, but he took no benefit under the will, which had not yet been proved.' He claimed again that he had kept no accounts – which caused the judge to say that Ellis would find it difficult if ever he applied to have his bankruptcy discharged.

Was Henry just a bad businessman whose alcoholic wife had died at an opportune moment to save him from financial ruin – or was he a heartless killer who poisoned his rich wife merely to save his own skin? We will never be certain – public opinion at the time cast him in the latter role but the provisions of his wife's will seem to indicate Henry's innocence. What is your verdict?

North Devon Journal-Herald 14.8.1986

78. HARD LINE ON SMUGGLERS

Much romantic codswallop has been written about smuggling in North Devon. The truth is much harder to come by as smugglers rarely wrote their autobiographies.

In January 1892, however, one Philip Hambly of Welcombe died aged about 80 and his obituary notes that his death 'has removed the oldest native of the parish and at the same time severed the last living link with the old smuggling days.'

In the early eighteenth century Marsland Mouth at Welcombe on the Devon/Cornwall border was the centre of a thriving smugglers' nest. The local Customs Officers kept away – bribed with sums of up to £100 a year – a tremendous sum then and indicative of the worth of the 'trade'. Indeed at times there were 'high carousels lasting all night' with the Officers joining in.

It all came to an abrupt end around 1820 when Hambly, then a young lad was 'appointed to the responsible post of horse leader' by the smugglers. This job meant that he had to lead a string of pack horses to Marsland Mouth where they were loaded up with small kegs of brandy and then take them inland where the spirits were hidden in various caves and farmhouses.

Everything was going well with the 'cargo distribution' but someone had informed on them and 'the officers of the law pounced down upon them' and arrested everybody 'who assisted even in the most remote way in landing or removing the 'mum' as it was called.'

Jail sentences and heavy fines followed but Philip was judged too young to be punished so it was decided that his father had to suffer in his place. George Hambly, as he was called, was convicted for lending his horses to the smugglers and sentenced to six months in jail. However, he managed to elude capture for the next year 'by sleeping about in different places and coming home to work by day' – which doesn't say much for the efficiency of the early policing system.

His pursuers on arrival in Welcombe would pass the Blue Fox Inn near the church on their way to his house and as they passed the publican would hoist 'a signal which could be seen at Hambly's residence' and off the hunted man would go.

Other men involved in the smuggling operation weren't so lucky, or elusive. One was fined £200 for lending his cart to the smugglers and two young men who merely helped push the cart when it got stuck in some mud were sent to jail as accessories even though they didn't realise they were helping smugglers! In fact, 'So much consternation and misery were caused, and many families ruined by this episode that no one has ever since made an attempt to revive the trade.'

Marsland Mouth today is a quiet beach popular with locals and tourists alike, but I wonder how many sitting there in the hot sun on a summer's day realise what stirring events went on there some 170 years ago?

North Devon Journal 7.2.1991

79. JAILED FOR NOT STEALING ANY CIGARETTES

'The good old days' – when everything was simple and life was good – or so we generally like to think. A criminal case in May 1908 shows just how rose-tinted that view is.

The case occurred at Bideford Police Court when the Mayor, a Mr Metherall, sat in judgement on a 13 year old lad. He will remain nameless as just possibly, he could still be alive. He was a local lad 'who was bound over under the Probation of Offenders Act to be of good behaviour for twelve months.'

This followed a very minor case of larceny. His probation officer – Inspector Francis of Barnstaple – had brought him back to court as he had 'failed to fulfil the conditions of his recognizance' – he had broken the conditions of his probation.

Mrs Harriett Davey, of Honestone Street, appeared to give evidence. She kept a small general shop and said that on May 9 between 8 and 9am she went into her shop 'and behind the counter stepped on the feet of a boy...who was lying on the floor under the counter.' Somewhat surprised she not unnaturally asked what he was doing there – to which she got no reply. She then called a Mr Paul Hoskins in and the boy got up saying 'I'm faint, I'm faint'.

However, he showed no signs of faintness. Mr Hoskins then took the boy outside 'and searched his pockets, finding a cigarette packet, three cigarettes and a half-penny.' The boy claimed he had bought the cigarettes elsewhere but a quick check revealed two open drawers behind the counter – which Mrs Davey knew she had left closed. P.C. Bastin took the stand next and recountered how he had questioned the lad who repeated his story as to entering the shop because he felt faint.

Inspector Francis, the probation officer (and the representative of the NSPCC) questioned the boy several days later and got the truth.

The boy's father had given him a half-penny for sweets and finding the shop unattended when he entered the boy crept behind the counter in order to steal any cigarettes he could find. Hearing footsteps he panicked and hid behind the counter. The cigarettes found in his pocket had been legally purchased the day before. No theft, therefore had taken place and in further mitigation it was pointed out that the boy 'did not seem to have ordinary intelligence in that he had been attending school for several years but was only in the first standard.'

Inspector Francis, however, asked that 'the boy be sent to a certified reformatory, as he was quite out of control.' The magistrates present obviously agreed and 'decided to convict the boy of being a rogue and a vagrant' for which they sentenced him to one day's imprisonment.

In addition and as a direct result of breaking his probation this backward 13 year old was sent to Devon and Exeter Reformatory for Boys at Exeter for five years. To add insult to injury the boy's father was ordered to pay 1s 6d (7½p) a week towards his maintenance there. The report on the case in the local newspaper is headed 'Incorrigible Bideford Boy' – an example of the 'good old days' to perhaps show that they weren't so good after all?

North Devon Journal 23.7.1987

80. WHEN POLICE CHARGED ON HORSEBACK

It may not seem it but politics today are rather bland compared to the past. As proof of this one need only look to the Parliamentary by-election held in North Devon in May 1911. Two candidates stood – a Liberal and a Conservative. The campaign was hard fought and nowhere more so than in Bideford long famous for its rough elections. The Liberal candidate, Baring, helped stir up feelings by coming to the town and denouncing 'Tory Lies' and suggesting his opponents were 'pub-crawlers'.

Then, as now, the final meetings of the campaign were held in the Market Hall. Here the candidates and their agents whipped up party fervour and boosted their own confidence. As the supporters streamed out into the town at about 10.45pm, however, 'a disgraceful and fortunately rare display of violence on the part of the Devon Constabulary was witnessed.'

To the 'surprise of the people', a party of mounted police 'galloped by on and off the pavement, followed by a number of constables on foot.' In the crowded streets their effect was devastating it was reported. 'Men and women were roughly knocked down and nervous people who had taken shelter in doorways were roughly pulled out.'

Even reporters who had been covering the meeting 'were thrown about from constable to constable, and were afterwards driven by a cordon of police out into a side street.' When remonstrated with the individual policemen would only answer 'These are our orders.' As might be expected 'frequent expressions of disgust were heard from responsible citizens.'

A few days later the mayor told the town council that he had received letters and complaints from 'influential ratepayers' and these were passed on by the council to the county police committee. One councillor blamed the trouble not on the local officers but on men drafted in from the country 'whom he might describe as crude officials.'

The county committee discussed the 'Bideford police charge' at their next meeting and heard the chief constable express regret that 'well-behaved people' had become 'mixed up with the rowdy element' and 'consequently came in for the rough treatment that resulted.' He ended, rather unfeelingly, 'They had only themselves to blame!' The Committee agreed and decided to take no action.

So finished the case of the Bideford mounted police charge. Just one extra thing – the Liberal just scraped home.

North Devon Journal 7.1.1988

ODDS AND ENDS

81. KING INHERITS OUR RICHES

Among the millions of records held in the Public Record Office in London, is an 'Escheator's Inquisition' of 1421, referring to one John Hawkin, a merchant of Barnstaple. These inquisitions were lists of property owned by those who died intestate (without making a will). The king received a share of such person's goods and these lists were thus drawn up by local tax collectors.

The list of John Hawkin's belongings begins (in translation from its original latin), 'Two horses 10/-' (50p). That John may have had an interest in some ship or another is suggested by his ownership of 35 yards of canvas, 20 flasks of tar and eleven stones of fine rope.

The main part of the inventory, however, indicates that drapery was the major item of his stock-in-trade. Various materials are listed, some with now odd names though others are still recognisable. Among the latter we find 'Twylly' for beds, ten yards of 'Bunting'. More unusual are the four yards of 'Carde' a type of fabric used for curtains and linings and half a yard of 'Bordalisaundre'. This should actually be called 'Bord d'Alexandre' which was a type of striped silk named after the city of Alexandria in Egypt.

One wonders which gallants in North Devon were wearing such exotic material? In addition there were silk ribbons, white cloths and even half a gross of 'points' or laces, used for both fastening shoes and lacing up jackets and trousers. He had a wide variety of other trade items, including 10lbs of white soap and one barrel of black soap.

The other major group of items in the inventory consisted of various spices and minerals, including pepper, cummin, mace, honeyed ginger, aniseed and even alum (used for preserving). Miscellaneous items ranged from the ten pairs of knives of 'Axetede-ware' (an apparent reference to a place in Kent), three daggers and twenty belts for boys with fittings of copper and tin.

More unusually, there were three sets of amber rosary beads and two other sets of jet. England at this date was, of course, still a Catholic country and such religious items probably had a ready sale.

Of John's personal belongings we learn little. We know he had a wash basin, two candelabras and two tables to put them on. This lack of furnishings suggests that John was a lodger in someone else's house.

I am unsure just how much of his estate went to the crown, but interestingly enough this rule is still in operation today in those areas owned by the Prince of Wales.

North Devon Journal 19.7.1990

82. COUNTING THE COSTS IN HARTLAND

Accounts to most people are dry things and not particularly interesting. When, however, they are over 370 years old they become fascinating. Hartland is lucky in that its 'Town Accounts' go back to 1612 when they were kept by the Port Reeve – the equivalent of a Mayor elsewhere.

Income totalled some £18.16.7 – mostly as rents from town-owned lands and market dues. Expenses were about the same and are closely detailed. Many are to do with the town's administration including the 2d that went on 'paper and wax bestowed about the Towne business,' the two shillings for the account book itself and the 16d 'for makinge and wryting this Accompt.' Other sums went on the upkeep of the town hall – 'paid William Deyman for a beame for the olde hall 10d' with two shillings going towards 'Reed and Straw to thatch the olde Hall.'

One outgoing was the money spent on the town clock. Thus 'five plattes to mend over the Clock' cost two shillings and one David ffrye was paid one shilling 'for mendinge the Clock.' Other expenses were odder – John Prance was paid 6d 'for making cleane of the Boochers Stoockes' – presumably cleaning up the butchery area, whilst Philip Couch got 6d 'to carrie earth and stoones to mend the shambles' or butcher's stalls.

In connection with the butchers it is odd to find 6d being spent on 'a dynner for them that brought Dogges to the bull.' At this period all bulls had by law to be baited or savaged by dogs before being killed – this being supposed to render the meat tender!

Another 3d went to 'them that made fast the somer Pole' which is presumably the May Pole. This ritual, a survival from earlier fertility festivals was heavily stamped on by Cromwell and the Puritans later in the seventeenth century.

Money also went on law and order – thus the large sum of one shilling eight pence was spent on 'Caringe (carrying) Anne Blackmore to the gaile' – presumably at Bideford or Exeter, whilst 3d went on John Leech 'for watching one night att the ffair.'

The single largest payment seems to have been the 1s 6d spent on 'bread and Drinke bestowed the Accompt Daye.' Presumably all the local dignitaries turned up to check the accounts and feed themselves well in the process – clearly one of the perks of their position!

The accounts continue in an unbroken run until 1713 and provide a tremendously rich storehouse of Hartland's history just calling out for some detailed work by a keen researcher today.

North Devon Journal 18.8.1988

83. PASS TO LEAVE A PARISH

Among the records created by the old Barnstaple corporation was *A Book of Remembrance*. It seems to have been a volume containing council resolutions thought worthy of remembering.

In 1628, for example, 'Mr William Palmer brought into the town hall four new leather buckets' – an indication probably of the rather basic firefighting arrangements. Also from 1628 we read that Christopher Thomas from South Wales, a 'vagrant person' without a pass, was given 10 days to leave town. Such entries are common and refer to the old system of settlement. If you couldn't produce the certificate or pass allowing you to travel from your home parish you were sent back.

Perhaps the oddest entry that year concerns John Gread who offered £1 a year to be 'keeper of the prison'. Local government officials today, of course, do not pay to be appointed but at that time the prison keeper could legally charge prisoners for their keep – and by overcharging and supplying rotten food make a handsome salary.

The next year saw Richard Lewis, a gardener, charged as father to Joan Waterman's illegitimate child and having to pay seven pence a week towards its upkeep. Poor Joan ' for her offence, shall be openly whipped about the said town of Barnstaple' – although what this could hope to achieve isn't stated.

On a lighter note, the corporation agreed to write to Mr Horseman at Plymouth to invite him to become schoolmaster at the grammar school at the wage of £6.65 for three years. This doesn't seem much but again the position let its holder charge pupils whatever he thought fit for their education. A note adds that the corporation could nominate up to 10 poor children for a free education.

Seven months later the councillors appointed Dr Symes as 'phisicon resident' to the town at £10 per year on condition 'he may give counsel gratis, unto such poor people and servants as are not able to pay.'

That the doctor's services might be required is shown by an entry in 1631 when having been 'credibly informed that there hath been a great mortality by plague at Bordeaux' the corporation ordered all ships from the French port to do 14 days quarantine before landing their goods. Anybody rowing out to meet any such ship was to be barred from the town for 14 days and jailed for eight days 'for this contempt and disobedience' – such was the fear of the disease.

In 1633 money spent on 'suppression of the Turkish pirates' was ordered to be raised by a levy on ships using the port facilities. These pirates, generally from North Africa, attacked shipping and coastal villages all around Britain, only releasing their captives when paid ransom money.

A rather different agenda to those of Barnstaple Town Council today.

North Devon Journal 3.1.1992

84. REMOVE THIS 'ODIOUS' TAX

The unlamented poll tax is to disappear into limbo along with all other taxes that seemed 'a good idea at the time.'

One of the oddest of these was introduced in 1696 and based in the number of windows each householder had – which made it easy to assess and impossible to cheat. A sliding scale ran from ten pence upwards. Our ancestors, however, began blocking up non-essential windows to reduce their tax burdem – thus giving rise to the 'blank' windows in old houses today.

In 1840 the Government proposed increasing the tax and a group of prominent Barumites quickly got up an all-party petition calling on the mayor to hold a public meeting to discuss the subject. They described the tax as 'obnoxious, inquisitorial and iniquitous' and were angry that the proposal had been 'so servilely acceded to' by the council.

This was strong language and at the meeting the mayor declined to take the chair because it was so 'disrespectful' of the government. A Mr Dicker took the chair, regretting the mayor's action saying 'when the House of Commons truly represented the people he should owe it veneration and respect.'

A Mr Trix thought the 'onerous and oppressive nature of the window tax was too obvious to need remark.' He realised the need for taxes but couldn't see any reason to raise new ones, especially as they had been blessed with 25 years of peace following the defeat of Napoleon. He suggested they write to Queen Victoria over these 'odious' tax increases and had prepared a letter which began with some wonderful language 'We your Majesty's loyal and dutiful subjects, inhabitants of the borough of Barnstaple...most respectfully approach your Majesty under an impression of the sincerest devotion and respect.' It finished 'we implore your Majesty, in the exercise of that benignity and justice heretofore so characteristic of your reign, to withold your gracious assent' to the tax proposals.

A Mr Young added that he opposed the tax as it 'interfered with the health and comfort of the people' in that it taxed both light and air.

A lone dissenting voice came from R. Gregory who thought it 'the least objectionable measure Parliament could have adopted to augment the public income.'

The meeting voted over-whelmingly to send Mr Trix's letter to the Queen.

North Devon Journal 3.10.1991

85. UNGODLY TOWN WITH LAUGHING SMUGGLERS

For many years during the eighteenth and nineteenth centuries the Government fought a hard and often unsuccessful battle against smugglers. One of the most notable areas for this crime was, it must be said, Devon, and within Devon, the northern coast had a fair share of the county's smugglers. The forces of law were generally insufficient to stop the 'free-trade', hampered by public hostility, government frugality and a coastline perfect for concealment. The law-abiding population must have been infuriated by the apparent lack of success against these criminals – not to mention the fact that their honesty was laughed at by the smugglers and their customers.

Two of these honest men were led to sum up their feelings in poetry and, luckily for us, their poetic anger was recorded in 1747 by the then vicar of Bideford, the Rev. Whitfield, in a private note-book. He was renowned for his public fights with many of his parishioners and these verses probably appealed to his nature.

The first is by 'honest J Gollens, ye Miller' and is simply a warning to those who were involved in smuggling – whether as customers or 'coasters' that they would face final judgement before God. The honest man however:

'...shall never fade nor fall
Nor at the work house feed
Provided still sufficiently
With this man's honest bread.'

Miller Collens denounces Bideford roundly in two other verses:

'As for ungodly Bideford
It shall be nothing so
But as the tide, which
with the wind
Is tossed to and fro

There fore the men of Bideford
In judgement shall not stand
Nor at the seat of Justice hide
The scale with equal hand.'

The second poem conjures up an even less pleasant view of Torridgeside with its direct hints at perjury and bribery of local customs officials. It was written by George Donne, father of the famous Devon mapmaker Benjamin. George was for very many years in the eighteenth century the parish clerk of Bideford and certainly would have known what he was writing about. His poem, begins with a sideways look at two customs officials – the collector and the weigher:

'Lord give such officers to the King
That we may cheat him well
And grant, that his collector may
In ease of plenty dwell.

And let each Weigher turn his eye,
Or touch the scale aright
And so defend from Equity .
The rich and rogue of might.'

Memories of old-style smugglers and their clandestine 'business' have not died even yet. Perhaps older readers can remember the tales they were told in their youth – though they will be the last generation able to do this as today's smugglers come via airports and Channel seaports far removed from the wild coastline of North Devon.
North Devon Journal 21.5.1987

86. WHEN THE PARISHES VETTED NEWCOMERS

Today we take for granted our ability to move house wherever we like. The only thing that stops us, perhaps, is the price of houses. In the past, however, moving wasn't so simple.

The reason for this was the old poor relief system where each parish looked after its own parishioners when they became old and ill. Because of this parishes were very careful as to who they allowed in. Newcomers were questioned as to their past and their answers were recorded. These 'settlement examinations' make fascinating reading today. One group exists from Winkleigh for the years 1733-1823.

A typical example dates from 1794 and concerns labourer Abraham Grater. He had been born in Chulmleigh where, when old enough, he was bound apprentice to John Kemp of Winkleigh. He served his time and married a local girl by whom he had two children. For some reason, personal or economic, he then left and joined the King's 'Marine Service' for six years, On leaving this he signed up with the Devon Militia for three years and then finally came back to Winkleigh.

A more unusual case was that of Thomas White in 1784 who, though living in Winkleigh 'has heard and believeth he was born in the Shire of Fife in that part of the kingdom of Great Britain called Scotland.' He had joined the Army at 16 and spent most of his life travelling with his regiment. He had married in Hampshire and had one child. No reason is given for him ending up in North Devon.

These two cases showed people travelling extensively. Another case, dating from the 1820s, concerned Thomas Goldman. He had been born in Dolton and was apprenticed, at the tender age of 10, to William Line, a tailor for seven years.

He dutifully served two years but then transferred his indentures to William Newcombe of Ringsash in Devon. He stayed three years but then 'by some disagreement ran away.' He headed for Winkleigh where he got a job with Abraham Reeve who paid him a shilling (5p) a week plus board and lodging for 6 days a week. On Sunday he went home to his mother's. After two years, he changed his employer, but not his wages, when he went to work for Aaron Hill of Winkleigh.

Just in case I am giving the impression that the examinees were all men there is the case of Penelope Hill from 1800. In 1760 she married Anthony Hill by whom she had six children. In 1788 her father George Packer of Winkleigh died and left her an annuity of £3 a year. A few weeks after this her husband also died and for the next 12 years she struggled on living on just her annuity but by 1800, aged and poor, she was forced to go to the parish authorities for relief, hence her 'settlement examination.'

All of this, of course, is small beer to the historian. But it is from details such as these that we can build up a picture of how our ancestors lived, worked and died.

North Devon Journal 13.7.1989

87. HISTORY LESSON IN THE RECORDS OF OLD CLOVELLY

Several months ago I wrote about the Clovelly churchwarden's records and a rare list they contained describing the village's poor. The records, however, contain other material.

Thus there is an 1825 list of 'candidates for boys' school', presumably one based in the village. We find Thomas Kinner, whose father was a 'fisherman and breaker of stones.' These stones would have been for resurfacing the parish roads.

There was also the 'boy Parsons', second son of the village tailor, along with his contemporary called Jennings who was working 'in Sir Arthur's Nursery'. This would have been Sir Arthur Hamlyn whose father laid out Hobby Drive around 1792.

Another listing concerns the Clovelly Church choir and orchestra (before organs were widely used every church had their own musical group.) Fifteen bass singers were listed including carpenter John Squire and mason Richard Jennings.

Against John Ashton's name is a note that he was a farmer who came to church 'about once in a quarter of that year.' His presumed relative Thomas Ashton has a note against his name, 'very nosey in voice.' Interestingly, no fishermen are listed, presumably their work with its attendant colds and flu didn't make them ideal choristers.

Eight trebles are also noted, all women.

A third listing deals with the distribution of goods and clothing to the village poor. A typical entry concerns the thirteen 'Black dreadnought (in) 1826 to Men and Women.' One of these went to 'Burroughs the Donkey Driver' which gives us proof of just how long the Clovelly donkeys have been in operation.

In the same year nineteen 'bed rugs of a larger size that the last set' were given out mainly to the poor women. Two years later four 'large cotton check rugs' were distributed, one going to Mr Bragg, another 'donkey man.'

One other list is of interest, headed 'Lying in Women who have linnen etc.' evidently a charity designed to provide everything a new mother might need. Four women are noted as getting complete sets of clothes and linen whilst another eight got just a set of baby clothes.

The money for all these charitable hand-outs would have largely come from the richer villagers and these records provide a good indication of just how important neighbourly help and communal solidarity must have been in the past.

North Devon Journal 4.5.1989

88. WHEN ILLNESS MEANT 30p IN 'LY-A-BED' PAY

Before the introduction of the NHS, most working men belonged to a Friendly Society to which they paid a weekly sum. In return they received sick pay when necessary and a small 'pension' when they became too old to work. Virtually every village had something like this – some places having several – and one of the most prominent in North Devon was in Bratton Fleming.

It began life as the Bratton Society but soon came to be known as the Bratton Death Club. This name referred to the formal burial it provided for all its members. The pages of nineteenth century local papers are peppered with references to this club, generally concerning maladministration of the funds and attempted fraud by its members!

It is interesting to go back to the original rules passed when it was established in May 1823, to see just how such a group was organised and what ideals it had.

Their first rule was that members had to be healthy. If you concealed any infirmity and were found out you were expelled 'and never again admitted.' An age limit of 35 was set with exceptions allowable only on payment of 75p for every year over that limit.

Membership was open to all except bailiffs, anyone who kept a 'disorderly house' and anyone convicted of 'treason, felony, sodomy or any unlawful action.'

All members had to attend a monthly meeting in the local pub where they paid their subscription of 2¹/2p plus 1p 'to be spent in the clubroom.' Non-attendance meant fines or expulsion. These rules were enforced by two elected stewards whose duty was to 'visit the sick', keep the keys to 'the society's chest' and 'give notice to all members to attend funerals.'

In times of illness, members received 30p a week 'ly-a-bed pay'. If you couldn't work but were mobile you received only 15p 'walking pay'. Stewards were ordered to check on sick members' health three times a week – no room for cheating. The only exception was if a member had a contagious disease, in which case a doctor's certificate was sufficient. A broken bone meant payment of 1¹/2p to the sufferer from every member.

These payments were cancelled if 'any members shall at any time be disordered by any unlawful means such as wrestling, cudgel playing, single stick fencing or the like.' One other self-indulged 'disorder' led to non-payment – venereal disease. Payments were also excluded from any member who joined the Services.

Any member who lived to the age of seventy got 12¹/2p a week pension and on a member's death £1.05 was paid paid 'towards defraying the expenses' of the funeral. At the same time each member gave the stewards 4p which immediately went to the widow or children of the dead man.

The rest of the rules deal with setting up a committee and annual meeting – with dinner and music provided.

As I said at the beginning, the life of the group wasn't smooth but at least it began with high ideals and a real sense of community spirit allied with self-help.

North Devon Journal 17.8.1989

89. ROYAL VISITOR AND THE FIRST 'WALKABOUT'

Ilfracombe is no stranger to Royal visits, both by British and Continental royalty but 160 years ago this year the town was host to 'Her Royal Highness the Duchess of Clarence.' The duchess was later to become Queen Adelaide when her husband became William IV.

She was on a trip around Britain and had stayed the previous night with Lord Clinton at Huish, and stopped for refreshment on the way to Ilfracombe at Lord Rolle's house, at Stevenstone. Arriving in Ilfracombe she was later to say that nowhere else in the West of England had she 'experienced a more respectful reception.'

Her arrival apparently occurred during heavy rain but it still didn't stop huge crowds gathering to catch a glimpse of the royal visitor. As the duchess entered the town the church bells pealed out, cannon fire salutes came from a battery near Wildersmouth and from the signal post on Capstone Hill.

Her carriage was stopped and, after she gave permission, the horses were unharnessed and 24 sailors 'dressed in blue jackets and white trousers' pulled the carriage through the streets. They were preceded by a band, waving flags and troops of gentlemen on horses. The whole colourful procession made its way to the house of one James Meek where the royal party slept that night.

The next morning after an early breakfast the party embarked at 7am on the *Comet* steam packet 'amidst the same enthusiastic manifestations of respectful and attentive feeling, on the part of the public, as that which had characterised Her Royal Highness's entrance in the town.' The public quay was 'covered with carpeting strewed with flowers and otherwise decorated in the most tasteful manner.'

The duchess was clearly ahead of her time as she did a 'walkabout' on the quay 'in the most affable and gracious manner.' She then boarded the *Comet* whilst her carriages were loaded on to the *Meteor* steam vessel. When this was complete both ships set off for Pembroke with the cheers of loyal Ilfracombe ringing over the waves.

North Devon Journal 4.8.1988

90. ARE PEOPLE REALLY CARING ENOUGH?

Today we are all numbered by the state, yet in the past a stranger could die in a place and forever remain a stranger. A case in point occurred in Barnstaple in December 1830.

The story was told at a coroner's inquest held in the Poorhouse of Pilton. Some weeks earlier 'a poor man between 60 and 70 years of age' came to Barnstaple where he was twice arrested and jailed as a vagrant. On both occasions when released he was given 'six penny worth of bread and cheese and beer' plus 6d by the mayor, taken to the boundary of the town by the 'rout beggar' and sent on his way. This strange title was given to a local official whose job was literally to 'rout' beggars out of the town.

After the second ejection the poor old tramp had once again returned to Barnstaple being found by a Mrs Corney 'benumbed with cold'. The woman persuaded two farmers to carry him in their cart to a nearby barn belonging to a Mr Vellacott. Here he was placed on a bed of hay and a servant of the owner gave him some food.

The next morning Mrs Corney took him to her house and gave him some food and bandaged up a sore on his leg. She then gave him some new shoes and a walking stick and off he went – back to Barnstaple.

That afternoon he was found 'lying near the road in a state of great exhaustion'. He was carried out to the Mermaid Inn in the High Street, put before a roaring fire and given some spirit to drink. The 'rout beggar' was called and recognising the old man asked the churchwarden whether he could be put up in Barnstaple Poorhouse. The churchwarden said no – on the basis that he had been found in Pilton parish and should go there.

The old man was loaded onto a passing cart and taken to the house of Mr Carpenter, Overseer of the Poor of Pilton. Here 'with great inhumanity' he was laid in the street where he stayed until taken to the Poorhouse. He died the next morning.

The coroner's jury expressed great indignation about the conduct of the 'rout beggar' though the coroner reminded them that their duty merely lay in deciding how the tramp died – by starvation or 'the visitation of God.' The latter was chosen with a rider that 'the inclemency of the weather' and the man's exhaustion were contributory factors.

A sad story of the heartlessness of some of our Georgian ancestors. The man was never identified and so has entered history as a lost soul. One wonders what his story was – that he could come to his death alone and unwanted – we will never know.

North Devon Journal 22.3.1990

91. DO WE HAVE THE RIGHT TO FREE SPEECH?

Ask newpaper editors what they fear most and they will probably reply 'a libel action.' We tend to think such legal cases are modern and look back in wonder at what our ancestors got away with.

In March 1833, however, a libel action was tried at the Assize Court in Exeter between William Thorne, a local paper maker and

John Avery, the editor of the *Journal*. The dispute stemmed not from anything published in the *Journal* but rather from a broadsheet produced by Avery at his printing works.

In 1832, the Reform Act had given the vote to many more men and in the first election under the new system many political 'squibs' o humorously insulting leaflets had been published by the various candidates.

The one that William Thorne had taken exception to was entitled 'Half-bred and jaded hacks to be sold' and was clearly meant as an attack on the paper maker. Thorne considered 'his private character was intended to be impeached.' He also charged Avery with malevolent feelings of envy against 'his prosperity and happiness.'

The editor defended himself on three grounds. Firstly, he wasn't the author, the 'squib in question was brought to our office to be printed in the regular course of business.' Secondly, he regarded the sentiments expressed in the leaflet as just a joke. Thirdly, he 'had no personal animosity against the plaintiff.' Indeed, Avery reckoned he had 'long promoted Thorne's business as far as means permitted.'

Avery did admit he didn't support his opponent's Conservative politics, but he did point out that both Conservatives and Reformers had been given equal space in the *Journal*.

Before a packed court in Exeter the evidence was gone through with only one or two new points being noted. One was when Avery's lawyer, a Mr Crowder, had to admit that the squib contained innuendos about whether Thorne's daughter was actually his daughter or not. However, when it came to Crowder's summing up, he reckoned the case to be a 'trumpery case got up for no other purpose than to enable one party to triumph over the other.'

The judge then summed up and reckoned the case depended on three points; was the leaflet a libel, were the innuendos proved and what damages would be satisfactory? He added that he considered it just a 'lampoon.'

The jury took their cue from him and after only 15 minutes announced Avery to be guilty and awarded damages of one farthing (about one twentieth of a modern penny), the smallest possible award. Such damages were, of course, a slap in the face to Thorne and a vindication of the right of free speech, though Avery was probably rather more circumspect in what he printed from then on!

North Devon Journal 19.4.1990

92. DO WE TAKE TOO MANY THINGS FOR GRANTED?

Today we take flying for granted yet the beginning of manned flight was beset with problems. A local case in point occurred in 1833.

In September of that year, an intrepid 'aeronaut' as he was called, came to North Devon. His name was Graham and he was a 'professional' balloonist who put on exhibitions around the country. His arrival in Barnstaple and his intention of putting on a display of ballooning was announced by a hand-bill widely circulated in the town and surrounding villages.

The first occasion of the intended flight had to be called off due to bad weather, but Graham confidently announced his intention of taking to the air on September 11. On that day a huge crowd from Barnstaple and the surrounding area collected around Barnstaple gas works, then sited near Barbican Terrace. Spectators were charged two and sixpence per head to see the operation.

Around midday Graham realised that he needed 20,000 cubic feet of gas and the primitive Barnstaple gas plant could only supply 10,000! He did, however, promise that he would ascend the next day, come what may. Many returned home greatly annoyed by what they deemed the deception that had been practiced upon them.

However, the natural curiosity of the crowd overcame this annoyance and they returned the next day. Again Graham announced that owing to there being 'some imperfections in the air bag', a large quantity of gas had leaked away, an ascent was impossible.

Understandably the crowd at this point turned nasty and to draw their attention away, Graham cut the tether ropes of the half-filled balloon. It rose up and disappeared, coming down later in tatters at Chittlehampton. After watching it go the crowd contented themselves with destroying Graham's luggage and packing cases.

Apparently the aeronaut did publish another proposal promising to make an ascent if the gas company would give him the required amount of gas for free. But, as the editor of the newspaper wrote, 'This we presume they be as far from doing as the public will from placing any reliance a third time in the professions of a man who has had the temerity thus to trifle with public confidence.'

Clearly it was not easy being a pioneer aviator in North Devon.
North Devon Journal 12.4.1990

93. SERIOUS RIOTS OVER BREAD

In 1835 the Government undertook a massive review of the Poor Law and how the poor were helped by the State. The old Poor Law dated from 1601 and was obviously totally unsuited to an industrialising Britain, but the changes introduced were not universally welcomed – least of all by the poor themselves.

The most obvious change was the introduction of the prison style workhouse, but it was one minor change that led to violence. Whereas before the poor had been given money in the form of 'poor relief' by a 'Relieving Officer' the new law ordered that they be given bread instead.

This led, in February 1836 when it was first put into practice, to two serious confrontations in North Devon. The first took place at Combe Martin. A correspondent to the *Journal* wrote that he was 'much surprised' as he descended Ridge Hill into the village to see 'two lines of Cavalry drawn up just at its foot – at the distance of a gunshot from the Town.'

This use of the military was unusual but was necessary as the local magistrates had attempted the previous day to swear in 28 special constables to protect the Relieving Officer. Unfortunately all but two 'had refused to take the oath.' As the correspondent wrote, all went off quietly but only because of the precautionary measures which the authorities had taken.'

The other event occurred at Sheepwash near Torrington where the local poor, mainly women, got together and rioted. Indeed, 'Such was the outrage and violence with which the rioters assailed the official' (the Relieving Officer) that the local magistrates called out the North Devon Yeomanry Cavalry to charge the mob and disperse it.

Five ringleaders were arrested and taken to Torrington jail. The next day they were examined by the magistrates. A huge crowd had collected in the town for this – many of whom were armed with clubs and the magistrates were forced to appoint a band of special constables as well as ordering the cavalry 'to be ready at a moment's notice, should any violence be attempted.' As a further precaution they ordered all the public houses to be closed. The prisoners, including a 70 year old man who 'wept bitterly', were taken off to Exeter jail by the cavalry.

A month later their case came up at the Assizes where the five, John White, John Brock, Thomas Pollard, Robert and John Balkwill, were sentenced to three months in jail after pleading guilty to riotous assembly. This sentence was relatively light for the time and reflected the peace that came with the acceptance by the poor of the new law.

Who says rural North Devon has always been quiet?
North Devon Journal 6.9.1990

94. CHEQUES OF SUSPICION

Fraud is generally thought of as a contemporary 'white collar' crime but it did occur in the past as well.

In May 1837 a mason named Thomas Kelly came to the High Street in Barnstaple and called in at the watchmaking business of Mr Alexander. Here he chose a watch costing £3 and offered in payment a cheque for £18 6s drawn on the locally based West of England and South Wales District Bank and signed by Francis Squire.

The watchmaker was suspicious and kept his client waiting whilst he hurried to the bank and saw the manager Mr Thorne. The latter immediately saw that Squire's signature was a forgery and, merely stopping to collect a constable, the men returned to the High Street shop.

After a heated conversation the constable and tradesmen agreed to let Kelly go home whilst they went to call on Mr Squire. When Alexander and the constable found Squire 'he immediately declared it to be a forgery.' Within a short time Kelly was under arrest for forging a cheque.

The story soon spread through the town and a local draper called Kenward hurried to view the prisoner. On seeing him he identified Kelly as the man who had passed a dud cheque in his shop weeks earlier. Kelly had brought some £3 worth of clothing and a hat and paid for it with a cheque purporting to be signed by one Philip Rock. On this occasion Kelly used the alias name of 'Thomas Barnes.'

Faced with this further charge Kelly broke down and claimed he had 'found' the two cheques in the street and thought they were 'good' thus making his crime one of theft rather than forgery – and one which, incidentally, carried less severe penalties. Kelly was committed to the town jail to await further investigation.

Come morning the jailer came to check on his charges and was horrified to find Kelly suspended by the neck with his pocket handkerchief, from one of the cell window crossbars. After immediately cutting him down the jailer called in a surgeon but he could do nothing.

An inquest was held the same day and it was noted that 'the suicide was most determined' as Kelly's feet did not clear the floor. Apparently he had got onto the window sill, tied the handkerchief around his neck and thrown himself off – thus breaking his neck!

It was recorded that Kelly had recently spent some time at Exeter as the main prosecution witness in a local burglary case and whilst in the city had 'formed an acquaintance with a female to whom he was to be married some day this week.' This implication that a woman had led him astray, presumably demanding money he didn't have, would have appealed to our chauvinistic ancestors.

In case you're wondering why anyone would kill themselves over just £18, remember that the average weekly wage of a labourer in the 1830s was about 40p – so the forged cheque was for a very hefty sum indeed.

North Devon Journal 21.2.1991

95. THE HORRORS OF THE WORKHOUSE

Mention the word workhouse to many old people and they will still react with disgust. In its classic 'prisonlike' form it dates from the 1830s and continued until some 40 years ago and over that time achieved an unenviable reputation for strictness and hardship.

That there was a factual basis for this is shown in many cases, one of which dates from December 1839. A woman called Julia Parker had been visiting her aged father once a week in the 'old man's ward' of Barnstaple Workhouse.

Although it was forbidden she brought the old man some beer and tobacco to cheer him up and relieve the depression and boredom of his incarceration. In exchange, as it were, he had given her his rations of bread and cheese that he did not want.

Unfortunately for Julia, she was caught leaving with the food and an empty beer bottle and taken before the local magistrates. They decided on a fine of £5 but as she could not pay she was sent to jail for a month!

This was reported in the *Journal* and generated a spate of letters one of which came from J. C. March. He thought the sentence shocking and blamed the workhouse governor for giving so much food to the paupers that there was any to spare.

This wasn't quite so hard as it sounds as he went on to suggest that the paupers be given food they would eat rather than food they wouldn't. His letter went on to discuss the proposal that the paupers be given beef and pudding on Christmas Day. The committee who ran the workhouse decided not to do this and March thought this iniquitous.

The letter ended with the warning that in heaven the poor 'will enjoy felicity in preference to the wealthy of this world by whom they have been spurned, neglected or despised.'

The next issue of the *Journal* carried a reply to March from someone who just signed themselves 'P' of Ilfracombe. This writer accused March of trying to score political points over the case. The Christmas 'treat' had been disallowed on the basis that the law said 'that the pauper should under no circumstances be placed in a better situation than the independent labourer or rate-payer.'

At this time the economy was depressed and many rate-payers couldn't afford beef so why should the paupers get it? A reasonable question but from just these various points one can see the beginnings of the extreme actions that developed and came to typify the work-house system and clearly shows why the place came to be so dreaded by the poor.

North Devon Journal 22.8.1991

96. A SAD LIFE FOR POOR

One of the most evil aspects of the old poor law was the parish apprentice system. If you fell on hard times and had to enter the workhouse, any children you had were automatically apprenticed to local masters. Taking on such apprentices was unpopular and the lot of the poor children was often unhappy. One especially sad case came before the courts in December 1841.

John Day of Newport, Barnstaple, a gentleman, was summoned for 'violently beating' his 10 year old boy apprentice named Bater who came from Swimbridge. He entered a plea of not guilty.

The prosecuting lawyer began by saying he 'did not dispute the right of a master to chastise his apprentice', but the master had to 'confine himself within the bounds of moderation.'

The boy was the first witness and he told how he had been apprenticed to Day about two months previously. A few weeks after-wards his master had tied him to a garden gate and flogged him with a whip until the blood ran down his back. This only came to light when Day took the boy to Barnstaple infirmary a week later and a nurse noticed the wounds.

Mary Ann Rudge, the nurse, said she saw the 'stripes' on the boy's back and extracted from him the story of how he received them. She asked why he had been flogged and the boy said a fellow servant told their master he had urinated into a teapot – a charge he denied.

Day agreed he had flogged the boy but not 'immoderately'. He had used a child's toy whip and gave him only 'six or seven stripes'. Not only was Day unrepentant but he reckoned the boy's parents, 'instead of complaining, ought to fall down on their knees and thank him for his kindness and attention to him.'

A second defence witness was a Mr Knox, a surgeon at the infirmary, who inspected the boy's back. He found evidence of flogging but 'the wounds were quite superficial.'

The last witness was Day's servant Maria Nott who gave evidence as to her master's 'kind treatment of the boy.' She was the one who accused him of urinating in the kettle. She admitted she hadn't seen him do it – but added 'He did not deny it.'

The magistrates then examined the boy's back and considered 'the punishment had not been excessive considering the boy's offence.' On this basis they dismissed the case. The moral here was clear. Poverty equalled loss of rights – whether you were 10 years old or 80.

North Devon Journal 19.3.1992

97. CUSTOM PROVES A GREAT SUCCESS

Today we are facing sweeping changes to our local government system. Changes are nothing new but date back to the great Municipal Reform Act of 1835. These nineteenth century changes were brought in to remedy widespread corruption but they also succeeded in getting rid of many quaint customs.

In Barnstaple one of these customs had disappeared many years before but in 1842 it was renewed by the then current mayor Gilbert Cotton. This was a 'Mayoral Aquatic Excursion' down the Taw in a mayoral barge. As soon as the idea was made public every available boat was hired by locals, both rich and poor, intent on joining the civic flotilla.

The day of the excursion dawned brightly and proceedings

opened with peals of bells from the local churches. These peals not ony heralded the entertainment but were also a celebration of Queen Victoria's escape, days before, from an assassination attempt.

At 8.30am the mayor and Corporation marched through the town and boarded their decorated barge – to the accompaniment of cannon blasts. The fleet of 50 boats then set sail to the strains of a massed choir and accompanying band in the leading boat which was under the direction of a 'talented resident professor Mr Edwards.'

As the fleet sailed down the Taw gathering new members as it went so huge crowds at various vantage points cheered as it passed and cannons were fired in salute.

Arriving off Instow they found the entire esplanade lined with cheering spectators as was the opposite shore of Appledore. Additionally all the ships in Appledore Pool were dressed overall in flags. Here they were joined by a large contingent of boats from Bideford which brought the size of the fleet up to around 100 which must have been a sight to behold.

Thus reinforced the armada sailed on to reach their destination by midday – Saunton Sands. Here they found a crowd of many thousands of people who had chosen to walk, ride or drive to the beach rather than sail including it was noted 'very many of the higher classes.'

When everyone had got ashore a giant picnic was held with some 4000 people; those who hadn't brought food were served by 'stalls of edibles, fruits and fluids' set upon the sands. The mayor's party were summoned to eat by a bugle call and ate 'in exquisite style' on their barge with 'a zest sharpened by the bracing air on the sands and the tempting quality of the condiments.'

The meal was accompanied by choice wines from the mayor's own cellar which were poured 'with no grudging hand.' A whole succession of toasts were then proposed and drunk, the first being to the safety of the Queen.

After a protracted lunch the whole party re-embarked and set sail back to Barnstaple arriving there around 9pm – to be greeted by renewed cheers froma huge crowd.

The Clerk of the Peace, William Gribble, then led a toast to the health of the mayor which 'called forth the warmest response which cordial friendship and esteem could give.' With this the crowd went home, the boats were moored and Barnstaple returned to its more humdrum existence.

I am not sure when the custom finally died out but it seems to have been such a success that one is tempted to ask whether the current incumbent of the mayor's office should bring this particular old custom back to life.

North Devon Journal 27.8.1992

98. BLAMELESS BUT SOCIETY FINDS THEM GUILTY

Discuss 'Victorian England' with most people and two things will probably enter the conversation sooner or later – religion and workhouses.

In February 1857 the two were also on the lips of every contemporary person here in North Devon. The reason was simple – a member of the Barnstaple Workhouse management committee had visited the institution and had been shocked by the inmates' lack of religious knowledge.

His shock turned to anger when he remembered his committee paid for the services of the Rev. Johnstone as workhouse chaplain. He demanded and obtained a special inquiry into the 'Moral and Religious State of the Inmates.'

In the male ward they found 22 men who had three bibles between them. When questioned as to religious matter the majority answered satisfactorily.

In the female sick ward were 23 adults and children with only one bible and one prayer book. The nurse reported that the chaplain came to read the bible on Saturdays but that she never heard him speak to the inmates on religion.

The nearby 'Oakum shop for women who have bastard children' held four inmates who spent their time unpicking old tarred rope into its separate strands known as oakum. The chaplain 'never visited them, they had no books and knew nothing of salvation.'

The committee went on to visit the Girls' and Boys' school rooms. here they found daily prayers and scripture lessons but both the master and mistress of the schools, however, had to admit they had never seen more than two religious books from the workhouse library.

The committee's report ended by saying that 'their opinion was that the state of things was not as satisfactory as could be wished.'

When the report was presented to the management meeting a long and very heated discussion took place. Two groups were evident –

the churchmen who supported the chaplain and the dissenters who wanted the chaplain censured. The end result was that the managers rejected their committee's report with the wonderful statement that it 'might reasonably have been anticipated, considering their (the inmates') character and habits.'

So it wasn't the chaplain's laziness that was the problem, rather it was the innate badness of the workhouse paupers that was to blame. This conclusion was condemned at the time by a large body of opinion in North Devon. It does, however, highlight another feature of Victorian England not often touched on today – hypocrisy.
North Devon Journal 5.4.1990.

99 QUACKS SELLING NOSTRUMS PUT UNDER ARREST

Much is written about alternative medicine today but in the past there were 'alternative practitioners.' These people, however, were generally 'quacks' out to part a gullible public from its money. In February 1861 two of these cheats were arrested at Barnstaple.

The self-styled Professor Robert Marshall and his companion Henry Hamilton had set up their carts in Boutport Street near the Pannier Market entrance 'from whence they harangued a crowd to whom they recommended their nostrums for the cure of coughs, colds, shortness of breath, pains in the stomach, worms – in fact, every ill that flesh is heir to.' It was whilst doing this that Superintendent Moran and Sergeant Chanter came along and arrested them.

At their court appearance, Marshall was described as 'a cadaverous looking personage, with bushy moustaches and a beard that would do honour to a he-goat.' His reply to the charge of obstruction was that he didn't deny 'lecturing in the street,' but said he had been given permission by the market-owner – a claim immediately denied by the owner who was in court.

The police then went on to accuse Marshall of 'exhibiting prints or paintings of a disgusting description not fit to be exposed to the view of females.' The 'Professor' loudly protested that they were merely anatomical drawings but the police maintained they were, in fact, obscene.

Seeing which way the case was going, Marshall sought to have it adjourned to allow him time to consult his London solicitor. The magistrates refused probably realising that the 'quack' would rapidly disappear given half a chance.

His fellow 'quack' Hamilton, described as having a 'scrubbing brush' of a beard, then appeared and claimed 'he had paid 40s to the College of Surgeons for authority to vend his medicines in any city or market town in the kingdom' – a claim ignored by the bench.

The upshot of the cases was simple – the men were fined £1 plus 10s costs each with the alternative of 10 days gaol. Both paid but Hamilton, as he left the court, 'had a parting shy at the Police' – for which he was very nearly re-arrested!

North Devon Journal 13.10.1988

100. WHEN PUPILS WERE TEACHERS AT 6d A WEEK

Nowadays just about everyone goes to school. In the past, however, school attendance for many depended on their ability to pay, though this changed over time as more and more communities built their own schools.

In Ilfracombe, Holy Trinity National School for Girls and Infants opened its doors in 1863 under the headmistress Miss Kingston. It was she who began the school logbook, now resting safely in the North Devon Record Office, which reveals what Victorian education was like for the majority of North Devonians.

Miss Kingston ran her school under the pupil-teacher system. Older pupils were paid to help the real teacher by acting as class assistants and monitors. In February 1864, we read 'Susan Baker (pupil teacher) at home ill. Paid a girl from the first class 6d a week to fill her place.'

Not only were the 'teachers' untrained but the syllabus was narrow. 'Numeration' was heavily stressed along with a little grammar and much scriptural study – for instance, 'Examined the girls collectively in Holy Scripture from the Fall to the Deluge.'

One other subject, needlework, loomed large on the timetable. Indeed the pupils produced a whole range of clothing which was actually sold to generate some funds. Thus in July 1863 there is an entry, 'Sold one shirt for 1s 4d (7p) to Mrs Colwell.' Other goods recorded include pinafores and shifts.

The only other lessons recorded are class singing and the occasional walk or church visit. Only once in the whole year is there any mention of playtime when in October Miss Kingston allowed the children 'to play for twenty minutes for good behaviour.'

Under such strict discipline one cannot envisage any naughtiness, but children being what they are it did occur. In May 1863, 'Ellen Brown left, in consequence of my placing her sister in the third class for the examination.' A week later Ellen's mother brought her back and the girl admitted being 'sorry for her behaviour.' Later in the year four children were sent home 'for coming to school dirty.'

Truancy also occurred and in January 1864, a wedding took place at the nearby church and Miss Kingston noted, 'A few children at school in consequence.'

In August the school broke up for two weeks for 'Harvest holiday.' This was the time when the children had to help bring in the harvest and a holiday was clearly better than mass truancy!

The first year's 'log' for this school ends with a slightly ambivalent report by a Government school inspector who noted that 'Miss Kingston has been working here under circumstances which do not allow her to do credit to herself', though he did add that 'the school has much improved under her care.' One wonders if this lukewarm report had anything to do with the fact that the school held 268 children – and Miss Kingston apparently had the help of only two pupil-teachers! So much for overcrowding in today's schools.

North Devon Journal 1.6.1989

101. GENTLEMAN AMATEURS OF THE THEATRE

The history of the theatre in Bideford has many fascinating episodes...not least that of December 1870 when newspapers carried an announcement of the first appearance of Bideford Amateur Dramatic Club. The group of 'gentlemen amateurs' put on a comedy and burlesque in the Assembly Rooms for 'the benefit of the Bideford Dispensary.'

These rooms were in a building that stood on the site now occupied by Grenville House on the Quay. The director of the company was one Horton Locke Greet who had a house in the Strand.

The resulting review of the shown by a Victorian equivalent of *Journal-Herald* theatre critic Frank Kempe, was kind rather than enthusiastic, beginning 'It was their first public performance, and it was therefore well patronised.'

To strengthen the company, at least one professional actress was hired – Miss Jenny Fountain of the Theatre Royal in Exeter. The critic praised her and especially liked several songs containing local references including one that went,

> 'O Westward Ho!
> O Westward Ho!
> 'Twill be a jolly place to go
> In half a century or so,
> When the railway is completed.'

The following February the Club gave a performance of Christy Minstrel songs in the Town Hall as well as other performances. By April 1871, the club was in financial difficulties and it was announced that 'It is with the object of liquidating this debt as well as entertaining the public that the next performance will be given.'

It might have been better however, if the club had cut its losses and retired gracefully. The review of their final show was vicious. Noting that it opened 'before a respectable but not very numerous audience' it went on, 'The pieces selected were those which only require the display of very little talent and ability.' The writer then got into his stride and ended with, 'The acting was bad, very bad: the provincialisms were glaring; and when we add to this the fact that the prompter's services were continually required and that his voice was heard in all parts of the room, it is not too much to say that the apparent neglect of the members in regard to the not very laborious parts in the simple pieces selected for performance was culpable in the extreme.'

Clearly Mr Greet the manager could not let this attack pass unheeded and he replied but rather damaged his case when he wrote, 'I assert that the critique of your informant is uncalled for, and in some respects contrary to the facts of the case.' Note that 'in some respects'!

A friend of the company wrote praising their acting ability and condemning the critic but this was altogether too much for the editor who vigorously defended the journalist and championed his integrity. The passage is worth quoting to get the full flavour of Victorian journalism at its magisterial best.

'In pursuing this independent course of action we are desirous not to give offence or hurt the feelings of those who differ from us; but we cannot, offend or please, compromise our right to animadvert (comment) on public characters and public events, nor can we consent to make our paper the slave alike of the world, the flesh and the devil.'

No doubt and Mr Greet was suitably crushed by this reply. Suffice to say the Bideford Amateur Dramatic Club disappeared – never to return.

North Devon Journal-Herald 6.2.1986

102. MAGIC MEDICINE FOR EYES, FITS, WARTS AND ALL.

That our ancestors believed many odd things is beyond dispute. Just how odd can be gathered from the following four 'medical cures' which were noted down in 1878 from a 22 year old servant girl born in Hatherleigh.

The first of these concerns warts and is well known and still in use today! One took a slug and impaled it on a thorn and as the unfortunate animal shrivelled up so did the warts. The girl who gave the information added that warts could also be removed if you stole a piece of meat and buried it in the ground. As the meat rotted so the warts rotted.

These 'cures' are examples of sympathetic magic, and, it must be said, sometimes appeared to work though this may have more to do with the powers of suggestion rather than 'magic'.

Similar to these cures was one for shingles. The sufferer had to be taken, 3 days running, to a stream early in the morning where a helper had to pick seven rushes growing by (but not in) the stream and draw them across the affected part. Immediately afterwards the rushes had to be thrown into the water 'that the disease may be washed away.' Again there is the idea of transferring one's illness to something else thus getting rid of it.

The two other 'cures' however, were very different and rather bizarre. One was for 'any affection in the Eyes of a Child.' The child concerned was dressed in ordinary clothes and then laid in a newly dug grave 'any time before the corpse is put in'! It was acceptable, however, to wrap the child in a shawl so that 'it may not be chilled.' One wonders what on earth the reasoning behind this treatment was? Interestingly the servant girl who retailed these 'cures' had to admit that her cousin had experienced this one but it didn't do anything for her bad eyes!

The last one was a cure for fits though what type isn't stated. A person of the opposite sex to that of the sufferer had to steal some lead from the window of a church during the time a service was being held there. The lead was then cut into three and bent into a circle and each 'bead' strung on a thread. This was then worn round the neck of the person experiencing the fits and, hopefully, they would be no longer troubled by them.

The servant girl had actually done this, stealing her lead from Hatherleigh church. The patient was her step-father and the 'cure' actually appeared to work for a few months but, unfortunately, the fits returned.

Such practices as listed here, of course, pre-date medical science as we know it and in any case were often all the poor could afford. Their success or not seems variable but if people believed in them they probably did some good – if only psychologically.

North Devon Journal 20.7.1989

103. VICTORIAN PUBLICITY MACHINE

Whether we like it or not tourists are the lifeblood of our local economy. The revenue they bring is now greater than farming and the tourist industry employs far larger numbers. It is therefore very important to sing our own praises in terms of letting tourists know what attractions we offer – thus explaining the thousands of pounds spent on advertising by the local publicity associations and tourist boards. Nothing, as ever, is new.

As long ago as November 1888 a meeting was held at Ilfracombe of the subscribers to the 'advertising fund,' supported by a group of local hoteliers and shopkeepers under the chairmanship of H. T. Besley. Its sole reason for existing was to collect and spend money on advertising the delights of Ilfracombe – then rapidly expanding as a Victorian holiday centre.

The meeting opened with the chairman reading the fund's balance sheet. Some £181 4s 6d had been collected and spent 'chiefly in advertising in about 300 newspapers.' In addition the daily temperature of Ilfracombe had been published daily for two months in the *Standard* newspaper – presumably the summer of 1888 was a lot better than that of 1986!

If this seems a slightly strange advertising ploy then consider what else the funds went on – '£3 3s 0d had been given to the owner of a panorama for a large view of Ilfracombe in his exhibition.'

These 'panoramas' were travelling exhibitions of very large paintings on rollers which were popular in the nineteenth century.

Another £25 had 'been given to the *Pictorial World* for a special supplement illustrating the town, with reading matter' which seems very cheap.

Finally a Mr Grover raised a problem that one senses had been bothering everyone present. He reckoned that 'it was comparatively useless to spend money in advertising the town if the railways could not be induced to accelerate through communications.' Trains from the rest of England to Taunton and Exeter were fast but the journey onwards to Ilfracombe was exceedingly slow and put many possible travellers off.

Mr Besley said the committee 'had had the matter under consideration and also the important question of obtaining a steamer service between Bristol and other places but with no definite results.'

Another subscriber reckoned the directors of the two railways which served North Devon 'had too great an interest in South Devon and Cornwall to trouble much about Ilfracombe.' We hear similar sentiments today of course but there was definite cause then.

Added to the report is part of the coverage the *Pictorial World* gave Ilfracombe in return for the fund's £25. It begins, 'Ilfracombe is always charming, even in a chill October' (!) so we must presume the hoteliers were trying to extend their 'season' much as they do today. The writer talks of 'bracing' stormy winds and 'wild and picturesque' storm racked beauty. The villas 'perched high upon the craggy amphitheatre...suggest a reminiscence of Cannes.' As a winter resort 'the place is highly praised by some' – I like that 'some' – whilst the pier was 'glorious' in all weather even though 'the surf dashes over the hardy pedestrian.'

This drenching is referred to as a 'health-giving baptism'. I hope the fund thought their £25 well-spent – perhaps the Victorians found such spartan things attractive. I'm not sure that we would today.

North Devon Journal 6.11.1986

104. A RIGHT ROYAL CELEBRATION

Recent comments on the Royal Family have shown that they are not above criticism – a situation very different from the second half of the 19th century when Royalty was idolised and all Royal events were celebrated with gusto. Such an occasion occurred in July 1893 when the Duke of York married Princess Mary. Every town in North Devon held celebrations and those in Bideford were fairly typical.

The morning began with the distribution of five pence to every person on 'parish relief', along with the best wishes of the mayor. Those in the workhouse were given a special dinner of beef and plum pudding.

An afternoon church service followed in a crowded parish church with the corporation present in their robes. Whilst this was being held, the entire complement of children from the town's schools were lined up two deep along the Quay. At the end of the service, the mayor led the corporation along the Quay between the lines of young people to a specially erected stand. Here he presented 1,500 medals 'struck in commemoration of the auspicious event' to the children. Along with each medal went an illuminated card bearing pictures of the royal couple and a message from the mayor.

With the completion of this ceremony the children marched up High Street to the Pannier Market to sit down to a celebratory tea of 'full and bountiful fare.' Also in the hall were all the council work-men and their wives and they were given a meal, courtesy of Mr Friendship from the cafe opposite the market.

Whilst this was going on the 100 strong Bideford Volunteers (the Victorian Territorials) were parading in full uniform on the riverbank to the accompaniment of their band. After displaying their prowess at marching they fired a triple volley as a *feu de joie*. On being dismissed, they joined the children who had trooped down to the riverside marsh or 'People's Park' (today's Victoria Park), where an afternoon of games was to be enjoyed.

The biggest event however, took place at 9.30pm after virtually the entire population of the town and the surrounding villages had collected on the Quay and the Bridge.

A huge fireworks display was set off on the railway goods yard (where the new houses stand on the eastern bank of the river Torridge) – the river 'materially enhancing the effect of the display.' During this the local rowing club took to the water in boats illuminated with Chinese lanterns and 'a variety of coloured fire was burned on the dome of Tanton's Hotel.'

As the noise and lights died away the populace trooped home, no doubt to recall the day's events for years to come, although they didn't realise the next big royal event would be the death of Queen Victoria.

North Devon Journal 28.5.1991

105. POETIC THOUGHTS FROM BIDEFORD PAST

Sometime ago I mentioned a Bideford author George Whitaker who published just one work – *Original Poems and Prose*, in 1895. I quoted from the prose section which consists of a series of reminiscences about North Devon in the first half of the nineteenth century. His poems, however, though perhaps not so obviously interesting have a certain period charm. Most are on national or romantic topics but a few touch on local events and characters.

He introduces the book with one entitles *Bideford – The River Bank – A Sketch August 19th 1894* that begins:

'Is it a fact that what I say
I'm threescore ten and four to-day?'

He goes on to describe the boats on the river manned by 'stout-built bargemen' and ship's crews 'with iron health' especially the 'Braunds of Bucks who rarely die.' In addition there were 'Maidens in their wherries rowing' – not quite the usual picture we have of Victorian womanhood.

A poem entitled *The Life Boat Crew* deals with the Appledore men who:

'Though the storm is raging so
It has never yet been told of
That your names are tarr'd with 'No'.'

Whitaker dedicates another poem entitled '*The Sailor*' to the lifeboat men and sailors of Appledore 'Whose common sense and courage have often been brought forth in the great work of life-boat duty – a class of men who see the works of the Lord and His wonders in the deep.' Yet another poem on the sea is called *Somebody's Child* and has the subtitle, *Whose remains were found washed upon the coast of Clovelly Devon June 11th 1893.*

One poem has a contemporary interest in that it records the 'Armada Service' in Bideford church in July 1888. Whitaker lovingly describes the civic procession with 'Our Riflemen none can despise' – a reference to the local Volunteers. The town's Police Superintendent also appears:

'Upright as a bolt with the rest
With cap and fine braided tunic
Rigged out in his new burning best.'

One other local poem is also the oddest. Dated July 1893 it is dedicated to one Nathaniel Cox of Appledore killed 'by the bursting of a piece of ordnance on the bridal day of HRH George Frederick, Duke of York to HSH Princess Victoria Mary of Teck'. The wedding was celebrated with gun salutes but in Nathaniel's case,

'Great guns were fired, but still there was one:
Whose fragments made known a story;
A widow now weeps with her orphans seven,
Midst the glare of the bridal glory.
Poor woman! She lives in tears and grief.
She is thinking of children's bread;
As he who had gone these guns to fire
Will hear them no more he is dead.'

What a wonderfully bad last line!
North Devon Journal 8.6.1989

106. LIGHTNING THAT BLEW A MAN'S BOOT TO PIECES

Lightning has different effects on different people...some revel in its wild grandeur while others run cowering for cover to the nearest cupboard. Here in North Devon we get our fair share of massive storms and they often bring much damage when they come. Luckily, fatalities are rare.

In January 1899 a storm passed over Torrington and a lightning bolt hit Beam House (now an outdoor pursuits school). It apparently first hit the chimney stack which was instantly demolished with two of the chimney pots sent crashing through the roof into the attic. Within the roof space the timbers were broken and splintered and in some cases twisted out of shape.

From here the lightning bolt split into two. One part passed through the end stone wall of the house leaving 'a hole just as though a shot had gone through,' as one contemporary witness noted. The other part went down the chimney, filling rooms with smoke, forcing open doors and smashing windows. The whole of the front wall of the house was cracked and all the iron gutters were shattered. As might be expected, these iron fittings were also magnetised.

The occupier of the house was a Mr Lake. He and his family were in the kitchen when the bolt came down the chimney. The room filled with a 'bluish flame' and they all felt 'pins and needles' in their legs. One of Mr Lake's sons reported that this event cured him of long standing rheumatism!

That no one was killed was lucky as only two years earlier a Hatherleigh man had died after being struck by lightning. George Crocker lived at Marshford farm. One day, during a heavy storm, he went out to collect his bullocks when he was hit whilst walking across a field with his hands in his pockets. The bolt of lightning apparently struck a hard, round hat he was wearing, passed through his head, down his body and out through one foot. One other feature was noted – his boot had been blown to pieces.

Such deaths are rare, but I can point to a fair number recorded for this area during the nineteenth century. If nothing else, such occurrences highlight our powerlessness in the face of Mother Nature when she decides to exert her awesome energy.
North Devon Journal 10.5.1989

107. OUTCRY AS MAN IS FREED FOR CRUELTY

It isn't often that North Devon hits the headlines but in July 1905, a court case in Barnstaple became notorious. Walter Bell, master of the Pilton-based Cheriton Otter Hounds, was charged with torturing cats. Two of his assistants, John Church and John Higman, plus local grocer, William Ashton, were also accused.

Bell had wanted to 'bring out the vicious nature' of his dogs and came up with a sickening plan. A Pilton carpenter, Blackmore, made up a box to Bell's design, 12 feet long, and a foot square in section. Once delivered Bell then got Church to buy cats at 2s (10p) each.

When he had enough cats Bell and his men set up the box and blocked off one end. A cat was then pushed in and two dogs followed. The dogs naturally attacked and killed the cat.

Luckily the local RSPCA officer, a Mr Duncan, heard of this and appeared on the scene with two policemen and they promptly brought the men to court reckoning 'that more horrible cruelty it was scarcely possible to conceive.' The case against Bell was very damning and his only excuse was that he had shot the cats first before setting his dogs on them – an excuse denied by evidence from a local vet.

The magistrates sentenced Bell to one month's jail; Church got 14 days; Ashton was fined £5 and Higman £2 – judgements which were greeted with applause from spectators in court. The two men sentenced to jail immediately announced they would appeal and their case was heard in October before a local judge.

Two lawyers hired by Bell launched into what was described as a 'brilliant speech' which hinged on the fact that Bell and the others admitted their crime but that jail was too extreme a punishment. It would destroy Bell's 'whole life for public usefulness' and it was his first offence. As for Church he was 'obliged to obey the orders of his employer' and thus wasn't truly guilty.

Amazingly these arguments were accepted and the judge reckoned the crime to be merely a 'misdemeanour' adding that a gentleman like Bell 'would suffer intensely more than a person in the position of Church or of someone not moving in good society.' A fine of £5 was given instead of jail and £100 had to be given to the local hospital.

The case, especially the judge's comments caused an uproar. The local papers were full of letters from indignant pet lovers and others who thought the case had been mismanaged. The national papers also joined in. The *Daily Mirror*, for example, carried a cartoon comparing heavy sentences for poor people who stole food to Bell's relatively light fine. After all, the paper asked, 'What is £100 to a man who can afford to keep packs of hounds?' It also wrote of 'a gross miscarriage of justice' and 'a flagrant abuse of judicial power.'

The members of the Cheriton Hunt didn't waste much time as they sacked Bell almost immediately and found themselves a new, and one hopes less hateful, master of hounds. Bell disappears from the pages of North Devon history as rapidly as he came – and we were certainly better off without him.

North Devon Journal 3.3.1988

108. WHEN TEACHING GIRLS TO THINK WAS A NOVELTY

Recently I was lent a battered old book with the intriguing title *The West Bank School Magazine 1912-45* containing 25 issues of the said magazine.

The small private school was founded in Bideford in 1896 by the Abbott family and stayed until 1954, when it moved to Sidmouth. The school magazine was first published in April 1912 and had on its cover 'Printed for Private Circulation' by Coles & Lee of Bideford.

This first issue was prefaced with a short history of the school and there followed a whole series of articles commonly found in most school productions.

Even this first number, however, had one item which demonstrated one of the school's main strengths – its forward looking and modern approach to education. In a report on the Speech Day, one speaker stressed the need for a knowledge of French and German rather than Latin or Greek saying 'Unless we English people paid the necessary attention to the teaching of languages required in commercial life we should fall behind in the great race for the supremacy of the world.' Ignoring the imperialist tone, this call for 'useful learning' especially for girls was novel then.

The second issue in November 1912 saw an article on commercial design and poster drawing as a career for girls and notes as to the fortunes of the (all-girl) cricket team..

The war interrupted publication, but when the magazine began again in 1921 it included a list of 'subscriptions' paid by pupils, which sent money to a 'deaf and dumb Hindu boy' and a concert 'in aid of Russian children' – presumably White Russian rather than Bolshevik.

In this issue there was a history of the school Girl Guide company – the first to be formed in Bideford, in May 1918. Details of a large rally in Victoria Park are given, plus a list of members among whom is the well known Bideford artist Sheila Hutchinson.

The fourth issue saw another concert in aid of the 'Starving Children of Russia' which raised £3.75.

A long report on the Debating Society saw some intriguing motions including the still topical, 'That Vivisection is a necessity' and 'That girls should play boy's games' – this one being won on an overwhelming vote. The same society also had a lecture by the town clerk on how Bideford was governed. The headmistress closed this by hoping that some of her pupils 'may one day sit upon the council, as women' – a wish that was, I think, fulfilled.

This very progressive attitude to education was continued into the next magazine in 1924, which carried a report on a debate on politics held due to 'general interest being aroused with regard to the Election.' The girls discussed the minutiae of 'Protectionism' and tariffs with the result that the Conservatives won the vote.

I could go on detailing the many ways in which West Bank School seems to have been well ahead of its time but suffice to say from the foregoing I think it is clear just how good a humanistic education the pupils received – an unusual benefit in the first decades of this century.

North Devon Journal 15.10.1992

109. POP MUSIC IN NORTH DEVON 1967-68

In my last article on North Devon's pop music in 1965-66 I remarked that 1966 was marked by the growth of folk music. On the other hand 1967 was the year of flower power when both hippies and drugs appeared in North Devon for the first time.

Locals would have been alerted to the new music by the visit of Pink Floyd to the Queen's Hall in Barnstaple. Advertised with the promise of 'Psychedelic Lighting Effects, Violent Colours, Weird Shapes and Tumultuous Waves of Sound' a ticket cost 55p – which was dear for those days but then you would 'Witness the most incredible experience you've ever seen!' Very unusually for the time details were given of their music including the comment that the song *Interstellar Overdrive* 'starts as a simple riff and takes a sonic and visual trip through the galaxies, visually and soundwise as unexpected as an interstellar trip should be.'

Other national groups to appear this year included heavier favourites. In June Simon Dupree and the Big Sound were at Queen's Hall to be followed in July by the Addix and the Pretty Things.

The same month nearly saw a major coup for local promoter Mike Deakin when a group he had booked months before shot to Number 1 in the Charts. The group was Procol Harum and the song was 'A Whiter Shade of Pale'. Billed as 'The Sensation of the Nation' tickets for their Queen's Hall apppearance were an expensive 62p. Unfortunately the group cancelled at the last moment even though Deakin offered them £300 to play – presumably better offers came from elsewhere.

Other nationally famous groups to travel to North Devon in 1967 included the Mindbenders, Zoot Money and his Big Roll Band, Dave Dee, Dozy, Beaky, Mick and Tich, Geno Washington, Georgie Fame, The Alan Price Set and The Move ('The Flower People who can hear the grass grow'). The most interesting visit, however, took place in October when Barnstaple heard 'The American West Coast Sound of Robert Plant and the Band of Joy.' How many people could have expected Plant to go on to become lead singer of the world beating Led Zeppelin?

With all these comings and goings one might think that the local scene was quiet, but far from it. This year saw ever more young hopefuls and ever more dances and shows in North Devon. Mainstays of the local circuit were well-established groups such as the Gordon Riots, the Lektrons and the Better Days. This latter group played all over the area during 1967 but by the end of the year had changed their name to the Albys and were off on a tour of Germany. Another popular local group to change their name were the Prophets who became The Essence and as such played many dates.

In April 'Barnstaple's fantastic new group The Steel' played their first gig at the Wrey Arms. This was the first of many shows they played throughout North Devon under the punchy advertising slogan of 'Beat – Sensational – Beat'. Other groups included the Package Deal who played 'Handclappin', Footstompin', Funky' music, The Theodore Watkins Organisation (with 'Films and Lights'), The Mood ('Devon's youngest group'), the John Morgan Blues ('Voted top soul band in France') and the wonderfully named Mostin Grumphutik and his Liberty Camel – to whose music you could 'Freak Out'. This latter group actually recorded a demo disc of a song which bore the unlikely title of *Good morning Mrs Polly Tickle*.

The most newsworthy local group of 1967 had to be the Warren Davis Monday Band whose 24 year old eponymous leader came from Barnstaple. In November news came that his group had signed a £50,000 contract with Twentieth Century Fox in Hollywood to star in a TV series designed to compete with the then all-conquering Monkees. Whatever happened to that I wonder?

All these groups played in the many local venues available and this year saw two new major discotheques opening. In January the South Molton Young Conservatives opened one at the Goose and

Gander Hotel which attracted 240 people to its first night. A spokesman was reported as saying 'We only want respectable people at the discotheque, and there will be people at the door to see that this policy is adhered to.' Within a fortnight the membership was full and there was a waiting list. Unfortunately, and for some unexplained reason the club closed in July.

Other new venues were the Harbour Lights Disco in Ilfracombe and the Attic Club at the Ring of Bells pub in Bideford. The most successful was Jason's which opened in Gammon Lane in Barnstaple. In February the owners applied to the town council for a music licence saying 'We want a reasonable standard of dress, we do not want to attract a rowdy element to the place.' They were successful and the club opened in March although they nearly closed in July when the Performing Rights Society threatened legal action unless the club staged at least one night of live music per week. The owners agreed to this and with constant advertising seem to have done well. The club often put on special evenings. In August, for example, they had 'A love-in for all the flower people' as well as 'A Happening with Heats for the Hippiest Flower Girls' whilst in September you could go there and 'Switch On, Tune In and Drop Out'.

With this increased competition for customers different venues offered ever more exciting attractions. The Queen's Hall put on a series of 'Mod Balls' with various competitions and prizes such as the 'Mini Skirt Ball' in May and a 4 hour 'non stop all action Motown Spectacular' in the same month with the added draw of 'Girl go-go dancers' At the 'Flower Power Dance' in the South Molton Assembly Rooms in September you could get 'free flowers and joss sticks' so long as you wore 'hippy gear and bells'. One odd attempt to attract people was tried by a promoter at Northam who hired the Kynd pop group who played (in December) dressed in Father Christmas costumes with 'Flash and ultra violet lighting' as well as free mistletoe and Christmas cards for those who attended.

It wasn't just live music that made the news. In March the Continental Cafe in Braunton applied to the local magistrates for a licence to install a juke box. The owners claimed that over 140 teenagers went to the cafe every week and 'they all want music there as there is no other entertainment in Braunton.' A licence was not granted, however, and the case successfully went to appeal in November when four of the teenage customers gave supporting evidence – including one David Brenton later to be a Mayor of Bideford.

Opposition in this case came from nearby residents who feared excessive noise – a problem encountered elsewhere in North Devon in this year.

In Bideford, for example, in October the John Morgan Blues Group was hauled up in court and fined for making too much noise whilst in Appledore the following month three members of the Kynd were fined £4 each for a similar offence.

Such cases were symptomatic of the backlash against pop music in 1967. The *Journal* itself joined in with an editorial attacking 'Hippies' with their 'over amplified guitars and drums' and 'weird clothing and flashing lights'. The following week a letter in reply claimed that 'Hippies may appear bizarre and eccentric but their beliefs have religious overtones in that they preach love, joy, honesty and non violence.'

The writer didn't mention drugs which made the local news for the first time in October this year when police found cannabis at a dance in Queen's Hall along with heroin the following month at Westward Ho! As to non-violence clearly it wasn't hippies who attended a dance at South Molton in November and then rioted in the town's Square afterwards. Local police were forced to use their truncheons in arresting three youths, two of whom were sent for 'borstal training'. A similar occurrence in Ilfracombe again in November led to the newspaper headline 'Beat Dance became big beat-up' following the hospitalisation of five youths.

If pop fans got involved in fights the 'folkies' never did. In 1967 new folk clubs began in Ilfracombe, South Molton and Instow to join existing ones and attracted a veritable galaxy of folk talent. Maddy Prior and Tim Hart appeared in Barnstaple along with the Yetties, Michael Chapman, the Watersons and the Young Tradition. The Bideford folksinger Ruth Smallridge released her second record in June which employed the talents of Dusty Springfield's backing singers Madeleine Bell and Leslie Duncan. Described as a 'Pop Song with a folk bias' the record unfortunately went the way of her first single. Local singers were prominent in the clubs including an unlikely 'Balalaika Trio' from West Down who played at the North Devon Folk Club in July.

These clubs were well patronised and generally popular though one letter writer in July complained bitterly 'I have attended two public performances by folk singers in Barnstaple, and on neither occasion could I hear one word that was uttered.' On that crushing note we can leave 1967, its flowers, joss sticks, drugs and pop and go on to 1968 the year of diversity.

The early years of pop music can be neatly labelled e.g. 1963 the Beatles, 1967 Psychedelia etc but by 1968 the coherence that had marked earlier years was gone and the fans were splitting into differing groups. The 'old' groups were still around of course, Billy J.Kramer for example played at the opening night of the Cameo nightclub at the Atlantic Hotel in Westward Ho!. The write up in the *Journal* stated that 'he's no flower pot man, with flowery shirts and satin trousers'. These early groups were now belatedly trying to become 'all round entertainers' in order to attract a new audience and it was noted that Kramer's act included a then topical series of musical variations on 'Bideford Bridge is falling down'. Other similar groups played this new night club such as The Mindbenders, The Fourmost and The Swinging Blue Jeans.

Apart from these four no other really famous national groups came to North Devon this year - probably because of the expense of hiring them. The nearest locals got to seeing 'name' groups was in May and July when one-hit wonders Honeybus and Unit 4+2 played the Queen's Hall and in August when the Easybeats appeared at the Narracott Grand. The archetypal hippie group The Incredible String Band were due to appear in Barnstaple in June but pulled out at the last minute as both members were exhausted after a U.S. tour.

Many other non-local acts did appear but they were hardly famous. Who, for example, remembers the Popees, Traction (a 9 piece group from Birmingham with a girl singer), the King Bees, the West Indian Tornadoes, The Perishers or the wonderfully named Surrealistic Pillow? Some of these groups' claims to fame were slight to say the least. One group called My dear Watson were billed as 'From the Far North of Scotland, Recently Returned from successful Continental Tour, Parlophone Recording Artists' all of which hasn't left any lasting mark on popular music.

To prove my point about the fragmentation of the target audience I need only point out that during 1968 North Devon was visited by 'The Rock & Roll Revival Show.' When they first appeared at the Queen's Hall in May the *Journal* advertisement stated 'Now the Pop Clock is going back to Rock.' Nostalgia is clearly nothing new! Indeed in August 'The 1958 Rock'n'Roll Show with Freddie Fingers Lee' visited the Narracott Grand. A decade is clearly a long time in popular music.

One rather unexpected visitor was Ravi Shankar the classical Indian sitar player who played with and taught George Harrison and various other British pop luminaries. As a 'proper' musician the *Journal* not only printed his photograph but also carried an article about him before he arrived in November.

If 'national' pop groups were less in evidence in North Devon in 1968 the flourishing local folk scene managed to attract a glittering array. These included Tim Hart and Maddy Prior, Alex Campbell, The Tinkers and Shirley Collins. In July Beaford played host to A.L.Lloyd possibly the most important folk artist in Britain at that date.

'National' pop names may have been few but the continuing vitality of the local scene made up for their absence. The Kynd and The Few played everywhere, the latter with 'their electric organ' for the first time at a Northam Valentine's Day Ball. The renamed Spirit of John Morgan played regularly in Bideford and Woolacombe. Another renaming saw The Steel change to the rather more wimpish Goodship Lollipop but this didn't prevent them playing all over North Devon. Other intriguingly titled local groups included The Cellar Rats, Great Expectations, Yesterday's Future, The Museum, Blitz and P'Phew.

In such a competitive world each group tried to outdo the rest in their advertising. Thus the Soul Sound Organisation offered 'Soul a go-go', the Hip Hooray Goodtime Band countered with 'Shake & Fingerpoppin' whilst The Crust claimed to 'make your hair curl'. One notable advertisement in March warned 'Watch out All Little Red Riding Hoods beware It's the Sensational recording group Peter & the Wolves.' The most optimistic claim came from the Midrod Ends from Plymouth whose promoter reckoned 'This group is so good we'll return your admission money if you aren't fully satisfied.' Possibly these local groups weren't as good as their publicity. Certainly a Torrington youth club group who called themselves Volcanic Eruption claimed that 'Having heard most of the pop groups that operate round here, we decided we could do better.'

These inflated claims were backed up by ever more extravagant attractions put on by the dance promoters at their venues some of which encapsulate short-lived fads of the day. In January the Wrey Arms in Barnstaple offered a prize for the 'best dressed Bonnie and Clyde'. A week later the Kingston Club in Combe Martin offered £5 prizes for 'the trendiest dolly' and 'most attractive micro skirt'. Not to be outdone just a fortnight later the Goose and Gander Hotel in South Molton put on a dance with an accompanying 'Go-Go Dancer' called Dion. The following week a 'Back Britain Ball' at Halwill saw the promoter giving out free 'I'm backing Britain badges and leaflets'. In May the Wrey Arms presented a 'Two Thousand Pound Light'n'Sound Spectacular - Direct from Canada's World Fair – Violent Colours. Weird Shapes. Psycho Lighting Effects – An Adventure of Tomorrow – Today?' Chittlehampton hosted a similar show of 'psychedelic lights' in September whilst a 'Mistletoe Beat Dance' at Northam in December featured a 'Psychedelic Christmas tree, lights and Christmas decorations.'

Discos continued to grow in numbers and in February The Changing Times Room from South Molton went 'mobile' and put on a show at Winkleigh – thus making it possibly the first of many later mobile discos in North Devon. Amongst the presenters of these shows were Dave Walker, an ex-Radio Caroline presenter Tony Kaye and the oddly named Mr.Kazoon who was apparently 'Britain's most controversial disc jockey' though why this might be is not explained.

As in 1967 there were various complaints about pop music and its followers. A headline in March announced 'Lyn 'Cats' to be cooled' following a decision by Lynton Town council to implement new stricter conditions on 'beat dances' in the Town Hall. In August there were complaints about noisy pop music at the Torrington Drill Hall (now the Plough) and at Holsworthy Memorial Hall, whilst in March the *Journal* printed a letter alleging that pop music was responsible for a rise in suicides!

In May the police raided Jason's Club in Gammon Lane over late night drinking. Seventeen people were arrested and fined £3 each whilst the owner Colin Know was fined a far heftier £59. The club, however, kept going and even presented the cheekily named group Glug glug glug a few weeks after the court case!

The oddest musical story of the year was much happier. In October the Sandpiper in Westward Ho! played host to the Barnstaple group Goodship Lollipop who boasted a temporary drummer. This stand-in (or sit-in I suppose) was 82 year old George Mitchell who claimed to be the oldest active drum player in Britain. Who said pop music only appealed to the young?

150

110. NORTH DEVON AND *THE GENTLEMAN'S MAGAZINE*

Amongst the many volumes held in the fascinating library of the North Devon Athenaeum is a rare, long run of the monthly publication known as *The Gentleman's Magazine* spanning the years from 1731 to 1908. Housed in a large wooden press they fill shelf after shelf and present a daunting mass of old calf and paper to any reader wishing to consult them. There are several volumes of indices but these are pitifully inadequate being merely an index to the annual indexes found in each volume, the latter in any case, being very selective.

For the reader prepared to plough their way through the millions of words, however, there are rich rewards. From the colourful careers of highwaymen to the scandals of Georgian court life, from the records of heroic naval actions to the reporting of new (and sometimes alarming) scientific discoveries, from the coarse eighteenth and refined nineteenth century humour to the notices of new books – all is here. The magazine is a miscellany of the wise and wonderful and the strange and the everyday. But – scattered here and there on odd pages and in fugitive references – there are snippets of news and gossip from North Devon.

For the last three years in my spare moments I have been reading and making notes from these magazines. So far I have only read through the first 25 years but even so I have accumulated a fair number of references to North Devon. In this essay I propose to present and discuss those references and although it will read like an olla podrida I trust that, in the words of the magazine's editor, 'It will both entertain and instruct.'

In British history North Devon has generally been associated with one thing – the sea. Its connection with the sea via ships and sailors has been long and beneficial. It is thus fitting that I should begin the essay proper with an exciting account of an incident in the war with France that was fought between 1744 and 1748. It concerns a Captain Alexander Ley and the story is told in *The Gentleman's Magazine* by the printing of a letter dated October 25 1744 from Barnstaple.[1]

This evening arriv'd in this port the Pierre and Marie, a French privateer of 35 tons, 47 men, six carriages and four swivel guns, capt. John Lacost, belonging to Morlaix, who on the 19th instant, met in lat. 51.15 about 15 leagues to the Westward of Cape Clear, the Newley of this port, Alexander Ley, master, 13 guns, 13 men, 71 passengers (Irishmen) and 15 French prisoners: After a few shot, the privateer boarded the Newkey with 30 men; the Irish passengers refus'd to fight, and staid on deck; on which capt. Ley and his 12 brave fellows retreated to close quarters, and fir'd promiscuously amongst French and Irish; some of the foremost of the French were kill'd the rest retreated: They boarded a second, and a third time with their captain, who took the dead Irishmen and stopt the holes thro' which capt. Ley and his people fir'd, then cut up the decks and threw down grenadoes and a stinkpot, on which capt, Ley surrender'd, who had but one of his own people kill'd; but there were 31 Irishmen kill'd, and 30 wounded. Capt. Ley had his shoulder-bone broke by a musket which he fir'd thro' the hole at the French captain, as he was cutting the deck, and which wounded the latter in the hand, and the ball graz'd his cheek. The captain of the privateer took capt. Ley on board his ship, and put him in his own bed; used the men very well, because, he said, they were brave fellows: The Irish he put into the Newkey's long boat, turn'd them adrift, being about 12 leagues from Ireland. There were eight French kill'd and ten wounded; several of the latter are like to die. On the 23d inst. the privateer made Hartland and Lundy, which he took for the coast of France; but finding his mistake, and being very leaky, he gave up his commission to capt. Ley and surrendered himself and people. The French captain is now here, as are the wounded; the rest are sent to Plymouth.'

Evidently Captain Ley was a tough old sea-captain not prepared easily to give up his ship to a pack of French pirates. One feels some pity for the Irish on board – one wonders how contemporary passengers on a boat trip to Lundy might react if attacked by pirates!

The magazine records much other local shipping news during this period of war. Thus on April 20 1744 *The Prescott* from Bideford was captured by a French ship and a month later on May 26 another Bideford ship captained by a man named Young was seized.[2]

The sad roll-call of lost ships continues in the next year when the following boats were taken; *The Revolution*, Captain Mill and the *Juliana*, Captain Spencer, on a trip from Maryland to Bideford; *The Swallow*, Captain Russell, from Bideford captured by a French man-of-war and taken to Brest; *The Vine* Captain Salmon, whilst sailing from Barnstaple to Viana, carried off to St. Malo; *The Peace*, Captain Hopkins, also taken to St. Malo whilst on a voyage from Bideford to Virginia; *The Resolution*, Captain Ley (though whether this is the brave sailor of the earlier report I cannot tell) overwhelmed by two French privateers between Barnstaple and Newfoundland; *The Raven*, Captain Walter, taken by a privateer from Bayonne whilst sailing between Maryland and Bideford; an unnamed vessel captured near Bideford whilst coming from Maryland; *The Bohemian*, Captain Harding, from Maryland to Bideford; *The Francis* under another Captain Salmon, whilst sailing from Appledore to Newfoundland taken and brought to Bordeaux; another Appledore ship carried into St. Malo after leaving Madeira; *The Leviathan*, Captain Nichols captured by a French privateer and taken to Morlaix during a trip from Bideford to Madeira; *The Robuck*, Captain Moore, carried into Bayonne whilst voyaging between Bideford and Maryland. In July 1747 the *Two Brothers* under Captain Peake from Ilfracombe (spelt Ilfordcombe in the magazine) was captured by a 'small privateer of Morlaix' though her release was secured by the payment of a ransom. Similarly captured and ransomed near Land's End was *The Vintage* of Bideford and *The Kent* under Captain Wallace from the same port. *The Dove* under Captain Baker was captured by the Spanish allies of France and taken to Bilbao whilst sailing between Bideford and Lisbon.[3]

When the war ended in 1748 one might be forgiven for thinking that it was not before time if the losses of the Taw and Torridge ports are reckoned up. It is comforting to note, however, that the lists of the ships taken during these hostilities are much larger for the French and Spanish than they are for the British. Apart from the incident with Captain Ley two other news items showed that local shipowners and sailors were not content to always to be on the defensive.

In 1745 we read of *The Benson Galley* (named after the local MP of whom more later), a privateer fitted out at Bideford and under the command of Captain Vernon. This ship carried 20 guns and 180 men. Unfortunately the context in which we read of this boat is not encouraging – it is in fact under the heading of 'Ships Taken by the French and Spanish.' [4]

A more cheerful note is sounded by a report in March 1746 when we read;

'The Expedition, (Captain) Smith, bound from Bristol to Jamaica, was taken by a French privateer, who put 18 men on board her, with orders to carry her to France; but falling in with the rocks of Scilly, and the Frenchmen being bad navigators, gave up the care of her to seven Englishmen who were left on board, and have brought her into Ilfracombe.' [5]

With the war over the local sailing fraternity settled down to the more mundane business of making money. That this could be profitable is shown by a series of pre-war figures relating to exports and their value. Thus we are told that in 1737-1738 the value of bounty paid on grain exports from Barnstaple was £543.1.3 and Bideford £272.4.4½. In the same listing the sum for Liverpool is given as £383.11.3. and Plymouth £753.13.9, so clearly the two local ports were of major importance in this sector of business.[6]

Not all maritime business was so honest.

Possibly the most serious crime connected with the sea and North Devon is also linked with one of its most renowned public figures of that period. In 1754 one can read an account of the deliberate sinkng of the *Nightingale* brig off Lundy in order to claim insurance money on her. The local connection stems from the fact that Mr Benson the owner and prime mover in the fraud was at the time Member of Parliament for Barnstaple!

The story came to light through the loose talking of one James Bather hired as boatswain on the ill-fated boat for a voyage to Maryland under a Captain Lancey. His account says that provisions and cargo were loaded at Boathead, near 'Knap' in Devonshire where Benson the owner lived. The cargo included 15 convicts from Exeter gaol under sentence of transportation to His Majesty's colonies in North America. Bather claims that they set sail but soon halted near Lundy and unloaded most of the provisions and cargo but not the convicts. After restarting they soon passed another ship whereupon the captain ordered the clearly not unwilling Bather to set fire to the ship which he did. The captain then ordered everyone to abandon the burning vessel and they were quickly picked up by the other vessel. This second vessel passed them to a fishing boat near Clovelly and they were then landed. After securing the felons in a barn belonging to Mr Benson the crew went to Bideford and made a sworn statement that the ship had accidentally caught fire and sunk, though this statement was only made after they had received IOUs for 'hush money'. Unfortunately for the planners of this crime Bather journeyed to Exeter and informed the insurance company what had really happened and in the words of the report in the *Gentleman's Magazine*, 'Benson who was member of parliament for Barnstaple, the principal agent in this villany, immediately absconded; and is said to have taken refuge in a convent at Oporto; his effects were seized for the king.'[7]

In later issues we read how Captain Lancey was arraigned and eventually executed for his part in the crime. Criminal MPs are not, of course, confined to the eighteenth century but one imagines that present day politicians who were planning a crime might be slightly more subtle than the evil Benson.

Staying with the subject of crime but moving on to land there are two items worthy of note. In 1731 there is an odd passage to the effect that a group of arsonists rejoicing in the name of the 'Bristol Freemen' had been captured at Barnstaple. It has not been possible to discover any more about these people or what they were attempting to do in the town.[8]

The other local criminal act referred to during the period under study concerned a gentleman bearing two famous North Devon names – Mr Chichester Incledon. On June 26 1752 we are told that,

'Mr Chichester Incledon of Barnstaple, Devon, was tried on an extraordinary indictment for forging a note of hand, for which he had a trial at the Lent assizes 1749, at Exeter, and had a verdict thereon; after which the prosecutor filed a bill in chancery, and obtained an injunction, which being dissolved, they brought a writ of error. And as the defendants, (the prosecutor's) last subterfuge, was to obtain an indictment, in order to ruin the man, he was, to the great satisfaction of all the court, honourably acquitted.'[9]

Clearly the unnamed prosecutor was intent on destroying Mr Incledon's character as well as his financial standing, though the court was obviously biased in favour of the defendant.

From the seamier side of life we can turn to the literary. Four such references have been noted. In September of 1735 an advertisement appeared headed

'PROPOSALS
For Printing by SUBSCRIPTION
a MISCELLANY of New POEMS,
On several Occasions,
By R. Luck, A. M. Master of BARNSTAPLE SCHOOL:'[10]
Details of this proposed publication follow;
'1. The Book will consist of 14 Sheets in 8vo and will be ready
to be deliver'd by Christmas
2. The Price to the Subscribers 3s half to be paid at the
Subscription, and the rest on the Delivery of a Book in Sheets
3. Booksellers subscribing for 6 shall have a 7th Gratis
4. Those who please to have them bound in neat Calve's skin,
to pay 4s per Book letter'd.'

These details are completed by the important and strictly
businesslike note, 'N. B. No more to be printed than subscribed for.'
If one desired a copy (and one presumes many old boys of Barnstaple
Grammar School would have been happy to buy one) then he is given
directions for purchasing as follows;

'SUBSCRIPTIONS are taken in by the Author at his house in
Barnstaple, and Mr John Gaydon, Bookseller in Barnstaple; and Mr
Edward Score, Bookseller in Exon; and by Edward Cave, Printer at St
John's-Gate, London.'

The last named in this list was the printer and proprietor of *The
Gentleman's Magazine* and it is interesting to speculate on his connection with Mr Luck. Such advertisements are rare and that there
was some form of connection appears to be a very strong possibility,
but what it was I have been unable to discover.

A copy of the book is in the North Devon Athenaeum and as a
specimen of the schoolmaster's verses I will quote just one piece.

'The Barnstaple Consort

Amphion, we're told
By the Poets of old,
Cou'd thrum on his Harp a sweet Ditty;
So sweet, that the Stones,
Danc'd a Galliard at once,
And settled in form of a City.

But, ye Musical Sirs,
Not a Man of us stirs;
Tho' Purcel you play, and Corelli.
If you'd please, you must treat
With much Drink, and good Meat;
And so touch our Hearts thro' our bellies.'

In his preface Mr Luck plainly explains why he has thought it proper to print his own poems and adds, 'This Candour I shall hope because I have endeavour'd to deserve it, from those Gentlemen, whom I have had the Honour to Educate. They ought (I think) to read my Performances as Favourably as I examin'd Theirs.'

Another notice of a book with North Devon connections is seen in the March 1756 edition of the Magazine where, under the heading of 'New Publications' occurs, 'Sermon at Barnstaple, Devon' by J. Baller, which was published by Dilly's. The Reverend Baller's sermon is not in the Athenaeum collection but various scattered references show him to have been John Gay's nephew. It is in fact on his testimony that Barnstaple claims Gay as her son. No evidence other than Baller's has yet been produced as far as I can ascertain.[11]

The third of these literary references is directly concerned with this most famous of Barnstaple's sons – John Gay. This extremely popular and talented playwright died in 1732 and in the June and July issues for 1736 the *Gentleman's Magazine* printed two epitaphs for him. Both give evidence of the high regard he was held in by his contemporaries. The first indeed is by the even more famous man of letters Alexander Pope and reads;

'EPITAPH on the celebrated Mr GAY'S Monument in Westminster Abbey. Lately finish'd by Mr RYSBRACK, the famous Statuary.

Severe of morals, but of nature mild;
In wit a man – Simplicity a child;
Above temptation, in a low estate,
And uncorrupted, ev'n among the great;
A safe companion, and an easy friend,
Unblam'd thro' life, lamented in thy end.
These are thy honours! not that here thy bust;
Is mix'd with heroes, or with kings thy dust;
But that the worthy and the good shall say,
Striking their pensive bosoms – here lies GAY.'[12]

The second is not in verse but is still a fine piece of writing. It was used to convey the regards of two of his patrons as the last section demonstrates.

'Here lies the Ashes of Mr JOHN GAY;
The warmest Friend,
The most benevolent Man;
Who maintain'd
Independancy
In low Circumstances of Fortune;
Integrity
In the midst of a corrupt Age;
And that equal serenity of Mind,
Which conscious Goodness alone can give,
Thro' the whole Course of his Life.
Favourite of the Muses,
He was led by them to every elegant Art:
Refin'd in Taste,
And fraught with Graces all his own.
In various kinds of Poetry
Superior to many,
Inferior to none.
His works continue to inspire
What his example taught,
Contempt of Folly, however adorn'd,
Detestation of Vice, however dignify'd;
Reverence for Virtue, however disgrac'd.
Charles and Catherine, Duke and Duchess of
Queensbury, who lov'd this excellent Person
living, and regret him dead, have caus'd this
Monument to be erected to his Memory.' [13]

Another form of literary reference is found in two fascinating short plays both written in Exmoor dialect. They both appeared in issues for 1746 one being entitled *The Exmoor Courtship or A suitoring Discourse*, the other, *The Exmoor Scolding*. Both are very light romantic stories whose main interest lies not in their whimsical plots or rather 'flat' characters but in the wealth of dialect used in them. The author who went under the pseudonym of 'Devoniensis' supplied a vocabulary to enable readers to understand what was being said. That this was necessary is clearly shown from this extract taken from the beginning of the *Courtship*.

'Scene – Margery's House
To Margery enter Andrew

And. – How geeth et, Cozen Magery?
Mar. – Hoh! cozen Andra, how d'ye try?
A. – Come, let's shake honds, thos kissing be scarce
M.– Kissing's plenty enow; but chud zo leefe kiss tha back o'ma hond, as e'er a man in Challacomb, or eet in Paracomb; no dispreize.
A. – Es don't deblieve thek, and eet es believe well too (Swop! he kiddes and smuggles her)
M. – Hemph! – Oh! the vary vengeance out o'tha! – That hast a creem'd ma yearms, and a'morst a burst ma neck – Well, bet, vor oll, how dost try, ees zay, cozen Andra? Ees hant a zee'd ye a gurt while.'[14]

The vocabulary supplied to these pieces is full of wonderful, and in many cases very descriptive, phrases and words. I have chosen a few to give the flavour of the whole and these appear below.

Bagged – mad, bewitched	Prill'd – sowed
Blowmaunger – a fat blow-cheek'd person	Ream – stretch
Bourm – yeast	Slotter – nastiness
Crowd – a violin	Strammer – great lie
Drumbledrone – a bumble bee	Totling – slow, idle
Hewstring – short breathed, wheezing	Vinnied – mouldy
Longcripple – a viper	Wangery – flabby
Ninniwatch – a longing desire	Wherret – a great blow
Peek – a pitchfork	Zowl – a plough

An additional selection of dialect terms appears near the end of the 1746 volume and amongst the range of words there is,

'Angle-bowing, a method of fencing the grounds wherein sheep are kept (in and about Exmoor) by fixing rods, like bows, with both ends in the ground, where they make angles with each other, somewhat like the following figure'

In addition to this interesting aspect of local history there is my particular favourite from these dialect lists – 'Trub – signifies not only a sluttish woman, but is sometimes masculine, and denotes a slovenly looby.'

From literature we can turn to letters. Mr Edward Cave, the proprietor of the *Gentleman's Magazine* whom we have already come across printed many letters from his readers on a whole host of topics both of general interest and newsworthiness. Most prominent amongst North Devon correspondents was a Mr Benjamin Donn of Bideford whose first letter appeared in February 1750. Mr Donn was obviously of a scientific turn of mind as this and future letters were concerned with mathematical and technical points. This first letter, after dealing with some abtruse numerical problems has as a postscript,

'The 15th of this instant happen'd a very remarkable Aurora Borealis, (but I did not see it) it was of a red colour.

The 16th of ditto, between 9 and 10 at night, I saw a northern light, of a white colour; a white stream of light, as in the figure annexed, apparently touched the horizon, about ENE, and extended itself southward about 80 degrees in length, making an angle with the horizon of nearly 45 degrees.'[15]

To see such a meteorological oddity as the Borealis so far South as Devon was indeed truly remarkable, even more odd was the red colour which I have not come across in other reports of this phenomenon.

In June of the same year appeared another letter from B. Donn recounting how on 'April the 20th between 8 and 9 pm was the most remarkable and beautiful phenomenon of an Auroa Borealis I ever saw; it rose about ENE, and extended itself nearly to the zenith, where it sent out rays forming the most agreeable concave scarlet cone; it did not continue about 3 or 4 minutes, when it became white, and dispersed itself abroad in various part of the atmosphere with a quick motion.

The quick of the scarlet appearance is here as nearly exhbited as the time of continuance would admit.'[16]

Clearly the publication of Donn's letters spurred him to greater efforts for in 1751 there is a long letter from him concerning Bideford Bridge plus a plate of his drawing of the bridge. In the letter he has several interesting remarks, one being to the effect that, 'the base of each pier is kept from accidents by a large quantity of stones, which are confined by stakes...' [17] On his drawing a small 'tower' surmounted by a cross is shown as being on the balustrade about half way along the bridge. This is shown in my drawing.

Donn tells us something about this long-vanished feature, 'The bridge has a neat cross, on which is this inscription; GULIELMUS ET MARIA DEI GRATIA MAG BRIT FR ET HIB REX ET REG, Etc. Hence I suppose the cross has not been erected above 60 years.'

Donn it must be who wrote the largest piece on North Devon to appear in the *Gentleman's Magazine* during the period under study. A correspondent early in 1755 suggested that subscribers in various part of the country might like to prepare an account of their home area with a view to its publication in the pages of the magazine. He went on to list a series of questions that could perhaps be used to form the skeleton of the proposed account. In October of that year an anonymous article entitled 'Some Account of Biddeford in Answer to the Queries relative to a Natural History of England' appeared. Although no writer's name is given I feel fairly certain that Donn was the author.[18]

The article covers just over six columns or three pages and is full of fascinating information. After dealing with the bridge and discovering 'many errors' in past accounts the writer goes on to discuss other points of interest. For example, 'The boats used on the river for hire are passage boats, ballast boats, and lighters; in the passage boat a passenger is carried from Biddeford to Appledore, three miles for a penny, and the hire of a lighter that will carry 10 tons, for a whole tide, is 5s.' In these days of diminishing petrol supplies perhaps it is only a matter of years before the ferry boat makes a re-appearance?

The author's opinion of the town is that 'in general' it 'is well built, particularly a new street fronting the kay, which is Bridgeland, and inhabited by people of fortune.' Commercial matters are touched on when he remarks that 'the herring fishery has failed for some years, and so has the manufacturing (of) rock salt into what was called salt upon salt, by first dissolving it in sea water, and then boiling it again.'

By this period the export of North Devon pottery to North America had evidently stopped as the only reference is to its export to Wales, Ireland and Bristol.

Bearing out the ship losses remarked on earlier in this essay we learn that, 'The merchants of Biddeford lost almost all their vessels in the late French war, but by buying and building have again made up their number to near 100.' We are told, however, that most of these ships lie idle 'as the hands that should have navigated them were swept away by the press, and others cannot be produced.' Evidently the Royal Navy press-gangs journeyed even to fairly remote ports to gather their less-than-willing recruits.

Three markets are enumerated being held on Tuesday, Thursday and Saturday. The middle one has now, of course, disappeared but the other two are still held regularly and provide both a social and financial meeting place between rural and town dwellers now as then. Bideford's housing stock is put at 'about 500' houses from which the author computes the population to be about 2500.

After writing about the parish church he moves on to discuss the non-conformists who possess 'two dissenting meeting-houses, one of which is pretty large, the number of dissenters being computed to be nearly 1-4th of the whole.'

Famous families and men are next dealt with and we read of the Granvilles and John Strange, the town's saviour at the time of the plague in the seventeenth century. An interesting sidelight is cast on today's inflationary wages when we are told 'day labourers have per day 1s, house-carpenters and masons 1s 6d, ship carpenters on old work 2s on new 1s 6d and the master 2s 6d.'

The writer does not limit himself to Bideford but also deals with the surrounding villages and Lundy. Of the latter he reports on its turbulent history and the fact that it 'is inhabited by one family, who sell liquors to such fishermen who put on shore there.'

In 'Northern Burroughs' (sic) we hear of the pebble ridge being about 'three miles long, of very considerable breadth and depth, so that altho' they have been long used as ballast, the number is not perceptibly diminished.' One wonders why the ridge is shrinking so rapidly at the present if, even in the past, pebbles were being removed.

Moving on to 'Ware Giffard' the correspondent lists the fish taken in the river there; 'trouts, gravelling salmon, flukes, flounders, eels, bass, and mullet' plus, in the tidal part of the river, 'bass, cod, oysters, cockles and muscles.' As if these were not enough we are told that oysters are also brought from Tenby (price 1s per 120!), mackerel from 'Comb boats' and herrings from Clovelly in such plenty, as to be 'sometimes sold at the rate of seven for one penny.' Clearly fish would have been a staple part of the eighteenth century North Devonian's diet – at the prices quoted it would certainly have been cheap enough.

Further correspondence from Donn touches on weighing balances, mathematical problems, the eclipse of Jupiter as observed by himself and Daniel Silk of Bideford and the transit of Mercury viewed by Donn alone. [19] In the last letter I have yet come across in 1754 Mr Donn was writing about operations on the eye. He was clearly not the only North Devon man to be interested in medicine but only one other reference to medical practice had been noted in the first quarter century of the *Gentleman's Magazine*. This concerned a Bideford youth who underwent an operation for the removal of a stone in his bladder. The item reads, 'April 10, (1731) Mr Cheselden took from the Body of Mr Hartwell Buck, eldest son of George Buck of Biddiford in Devonshire Esq; a large stone of 7 inches and a half round, weighing five ounces and a half In the Space of a Minute.'[20] Such stones, although not of this size, were common in the eighteenth century when food was often impure and diet in any case fairly restricted. The operation for the stone, as Pepys makes clear in his *Diaries* was one to be feared but was at least possible unlike many other types of surgery where shock and not lack of skill was the major killer.

In addition to all the foregoing human activity in North Devon we can turn to 'Acts of God' as the insurance companies would put it. In July 1747 Devon experienced 'Several shocks of an earthquake, attended with a considerable noise, and succeeded by clasps of thunder...'[21] This was a very unusual event for such a geologically stable area as Devon. A more usual occurrence was that recorded in 1749 when on February 5th we read that 'At South Molton, Devonshire, a fire consumed the house of one Mr Korslake, himself, his wife, deliver'd that day of a child, 3 other children, and a maid perishing in the flames.'[22]

Fire was an ever present hazard in the villages and towns of that period. The prevalence of thatch for roofs and great use made of wood in buildings provided ideal conditions for fast-spreading fires and it is a wonder so few accidents are reported. Devon, in fact, appears to have escaped relatively lightly when one reads of fires burning up to a half or more of towns and settlements in other parts of Britain during these years.

To finish this review of North Devon references in the *Gentleman's Magazine* we need to discuss the scattered notes concerning individuals. Most of these fall into the category of Bankrupts. Every month at the back of the magazine there was a list of tradesmen who had been declared bankrupt and amongst these were a few from North Devon.

Thus in 1736 Charles Standish of Barnstaple, a maltster, appeared in these lists. In 1742 a man bearing a notable and still current local name appeared – John Webber, said to be a maltmaker and grocer of Barnstaple. The year 1748 saw the appearance of a Barnstaple woman grocer – Katharine Hume. Two years later William Harris a Barnstaple carpenter joined her on the lists and four years after that a chapman or general dealer of Bideford, one James Schofield was also declared bankrupt.[23]

Turning from these economic failures we can read of the death of Richard Parmeter who was a barrister-at-law but interests us in his role as recorder of Barnstaple as well as Tiverton. His death on June 4th is recorded in the 1756 volume.[24]

I have now covered all the references concerning North Devon in the first quarter-century of the *Gentleman's Magazine* (one major story not covered here was recounted in *North Devon History* p184) and as can be seen, they cover a huge range from maritime history to chilling medical operations and from crime to literature, Hopefully my work will continue and many more such items will be located and added to my notes. With something approaching three hundred volumes yet to read (the later years being so large that two volumes were needed annually) there is clearly going to be a much greater collection eventually but this will not be for many years to come. Although not of huge significance in themselves these references do, I feel, add to our store of knowledge and understanding of the past in North Devon – a valuable gain in itself – but even more so if it can be a source of inspiration to others to pursue source materials of different kinds and produce their own collections. I can only close by saying that the reading of these old volumes has been a source of great enjoyment to me and I can recommend it to anyone.

REFERENCES FOR 110

1. 1744 p.616
2. 1744 pp.
3. 1745 pp. 80, 263, 352, 692, 696
   1746 pp. 63, 64, 348
   1747 pp. 91, 235, 335, 430, 483
   1748 pp. 128, 323
4. 1745 p. 49
5. 1746 p. 163
6. 1742 p. 140
7. 1754 pp. 176, 247, 278
8. 1731 p. 24
9. 1752 p. 33
10. 1733 p. 561
11. 1756 p. 139
12. 1736 p. 348
13. 1736 p. 425
14. 1746 pp. 297, 352, 405
15. 1750 p. 112
16. 1750 p. 269
17. 1751 pp. 296, 313
18. 1755 p. 445
19. 1751 pp.504, 563
    1752 p. 309
    1753 pp. 211, 428
    1754 pp. 458, 591
20. 1731 p. 172
21. 1747 p. 341
22. 1749 p. 88
23. 1736 p. 112
    1742 p. 51
    1748 p. 573
    1754 p. 96
24. 1756 p. 314

REFERENCES

1. North Devon Record Office (NDRO) - Parkham Parish Register
2. *Devon & Cornwall Record Society* Vol.11 1966
3. NDRO 596A/PO1
4. North Devon Journal (NDJ) 29.3.1832 4c + NDRO - Marwood Parish
   Register
5. NDJ 28.6.1841 2f & 3c, 2.9.1841 3e
6. NDJ 21.6.1849 4e & 5a
7. NDJ 28.2.1850 5a
8. NDJ 10.0.1863 6b-c
9. NDRO - 1851 Census
10. *A Walk from London to Land's End and Back* by Elihu Burritt
    (2nd ed. 1868)
11. NDJ 6.2.1873 8d, 13.2.1873 3d
12. NDJ 1.5.1873 8a-b
13. NDJ 18.9.1873 5d
14. NDJ 20.5.1880 2a
15. *Transactions of the Devonshire Association* (TDA) Vol.18 1886 p.104 +
    NDJ 3.6.1886 2e
16. NDJ 4.6.1891 2d
17. TDA Vol.57 1925 pp.115-6, 119
18. NDJ 19.10.1911 6d
19. *Barnstaple Records* Vols. 1 & 2 by J.Chanter & T.Wainwright (1900) +
    NDJ 15.4.1825 4d
20. *The Place Names of Devon* Pt.1 English Place Names Society (1931)
21. Devon Record Office (DRO) Devon Quarter Sessions 43/54/1-15
22. *Barnstaple. A Poem* by Rev.Richard Taprell (1806)
23. NDJ 1.9.1831 1e
24. NDJ 3.5.1832 4b-c
25. NDJ 30.1.1840 3b
26. NDJ 11.11.1841 3b
27. North Devon Athenaeum (NDA) - Harper Notebooks + various
    Directories
28. NDJ 29.11.1849 5b-e
29. NDJ 28.5.1891 5d, 4.6.1891 6a-c
30. NDJ 11.8.1892 5a, 8b-d
31. NDJ 15.11.1894 5c-f
32. NDJ 13.9.1894 8c
33. NDJ 7.3.1912 5e
34. NDJ 28.1.1926 8b

35. TDA Vol.71 1939 pp.249-265
36. NDRO 2973
37. NDJ 4.8.1836 4b
38. NDJ 16.3.1848 , 20.4.1848
39. *Hansard's Parliamentary Debates* Vol.39 p.550 22.2.1819
40. NDA Box 11
41. NDA holds a copy of the *Art Journal* for 7.8.1909
42. NDJ 12.8.1926 5a-c
43. DRO - Chanter index
44. NDRO 2532 + 74/5/1-13
45. NDRO - Tawstock Parish Register
46. DRO - Chanter index
47. DRO PR362-364 2/1,3,5,12
48. DRO Basket A/2749
49. TDA Vol.36 1904 pp.226-256
50. DRO - Consistory Court Papers
51. NDRO 2734 D/1
52. NDJ 3.12.1829 1b
53. NDJ 12.6.1867 7a-c
54. *Barnstaple and the Northern Part of Devonshire during the Great Civil War 1642-46* by R.W.Cotton (1889)
55. NDJ 26.1.1832 4b, 16.2.1832 4b
56. NDJ 21.12.1854 5d, 10.5.1855 8a
57. NDJ - various issues for August 1914
58. Oh dear - I can't find my original reference!
59. NDJ 24.7.1919 2c-g
60. Borough Council Minutes are held in Bideford Library
61. NDJ 12.11.1840 3b, 19.11.1840 3c
62. NDJ 27.10.1898 6b, 10.11.1898 2c
63. NDJ 18.10.1923 7e-g
64. The volume is still held in the offices of Bazeley, Barnes & Bazeley
65. *Crown Pleas of the Devon Eyre of 1238* edited by Henry Summerson (Devon & Cornwall Record Society Vol.28)
66. *Barnstaple Records* Vol.1 by J.Chanter & T.Wainwright (1900) p.172
67. NDJ 18.3.1841 3a
68. NDJ 4.5.1827 4c
69. NDJ 28.10.1830 4b
70. NDJ 4.12.1834 4b
71. NDJ 21.1.1825, 15.8.1839
72. NDJ 4.7.1839 2b, 16.4.1840 3a-e
73. NDJ 29.10.1840 2f-3a

74. NDJ 25.3.1841 4b-c
75. NDJ 14.4.1859 8e
76. NDJ 9.1.1868 5e
77. NDJ 6.10.1887 6d, 17.11.1887 6d, 15.12.1887 6d, 17.11.1887 2b-c,5e, 24.11.1887 8b-c, 29.12.1887 3a
78. NDJ 4.2.1892 3c
79. NDJ 21.5.1908 6a
80. NDJ 11.5.1911 6c
81. Public Record Office. Inquisitions Post Mortem E149
82. NDRO 1201A/B1
83. *Barnstaple Records Supplementary No.2* by J.Chanter - held in NDA
84. NDJ 11.6.1840 2f-3a
85. NDRO 799A/PI 125
86. NDRO 2989A/PO45 109
87. NDRO 1058A/PW2
88. NDA holds the original manuscript history
89. NDJ 7.8.1828 4c
90. NDJ 2.12.1830 4b
91. NDJ 21.3.1833 3e,4a
92. NDJ 19.9.1833 4b
93. NDJ 18.2.1836 4d, 25.2.1836 4b
94. NDJ 11.5.1837 4b
95. NDJ 19.12.1839 3a
96. NDJ 16.12.1841 3b-c
97. NDJ 30.6.1842 2f,3a
98. NDJ 5.2.1857 4b
99. NDJ 28.2.1861 5c
100. NDRO 2314C
101. Bideford Gazette 29.11.1870 4g, 16.5.1871 4b, 23.5.1871 4b.
102. TDA Vol.10 1878 pp.101-103
103. NDJ 8.11.1888 2e
104. NDJ 13.7.1893 2a-e
105. *Original Poems and Prose* by George Whitaker (1895)
106. NDRO - Hatherleigh Parish Register Burials 30.4.1897
107. NDJ 27.7.1905 2a-c
108. NDRO B258
109. NDJ - various issues 1967-8

INDEX